W♦man

God's Plan
not
Man's Tradition

by Joanne Krupp

PREPARING
THE WAY
Publishers

*"Making ready a
people for the Lord."*
Luke 1:17

**2121 Barnes Avenue SE
Salem, OR 97306 USA**

Copyright © 1999
by
Joanne Krupp

First Printing, September 1999

Published by

**2121 Barnes Avenue SE
Salem, OR 97306 USA**

Permission to translate this book in its entirety into
other languages will be granted by the author upon request to:
Joanne Krupp, 2121 Barnes Avenue SE, Salem, OR 97306-1096, USA;
telephone 503/585-4054, fax 503/375-8401, e-mail kruppnj@open.org.

ISBN 1-929451-00-8

Library of Congress Catalog Card Number 99-93397

Printed in the United States of America

Dedication

To my girls
Beth, Wenda, Jamie, Kelly, and Allison

It is my prayer that this book will contribute to your being able to enjoy womanhood as God planned it.

Acknowledgments

First of all, I am so grateful to the Lord for opening this whole subject to me in His Word and for the clear leading He gave me to put it into a book. I am also very grateful to the late Mary Riordan who sent us the first book on this subject.

Next, I wish to express my deep gratitude to my dear husband Nate for his unfailing encouragement which served to spur me on to the completion of this task. He also spent many hours going over the manuscript editorially and coordinated the production. Without him this assignment would have been almost beyond my reach.

I also wish to express my thanks to our son Gerry and daughter Beth for the confidence they showed in their Mom to complete such a task. Their "sure you can do it" attitude was of immeasurable encouragement.

I am deeply grateful for those who showed early and continued enthusiasm for the book as they read through the manuscript at its different stages of development and for all the constructive criticism and suggestions they gave me: Evelyn Allen, Sandy Allen, Beth Bachran, Pete and Bev Caruso, Sidney Dosh, Jr., Irene Faver, Jay Ferris, Victoria Fink, Arlene Hughes, Bob Iddings, Charleen Knoch, Gerry Krupp, Tony Mader, Robbie and Jean Moule, Georgia Penniman, Carol Preston, the late Hans Schnabel, and Sylvia Zook.

I'm especially grateful to Treena Kerr who went far beyond the call of duty in preparing to write the Foreword. Her encouragement included sharing with me some of her own unpublished work on the subject. Her diligent reading of the manuscript was, indeed, a labor of love.

Heartfelt thanks to George Moser and his late wife JoAnne for the new computer they provided while I was working on this book. What a blessing! I also wish to thank Dave Hooten who helped transfer the manuscript from the old computer discs to the new. And special blessings to my son-in-law Greg Bachran and Lane Witt who both helped me keep my sanity while learning the new computer. They spent literally hours at my side or over the phone giving me instructions.

Many thanks to our friends Tony and Kathy Mader who, upon reading the book, wanted to finance the publishing of it. We are so grateful to them. And it has been a joy to work with Clint and Judy Crittenden in the final text preparation and cover design.

I am truly indebted to those scholars who have blazed the trail in study and writing on the whole women's issue from a non-traditional vantage point (see Bibliography). They made my task so much easier.

Foreword

Graham and I have known Joanne and her husband Nate as a couple since 1978. In our opinion, Joanne is one of the most feminine women we have known, for in all that time she has never been anything but honoring to Nate. She may have strong opinions, which she will always voice, yet she combines her words with both humility and submissiveness.

Woman is strong in opinions, but the writer has ample support from nothing less than the Word of God. To honor Joanne's request for input, I have read this book twice. This committment has been both a joy and a learning curve for me. The obvious care to biblical correctness and the desire to be understood and non-judgmental has been accomplished by much sweat and tears. The grace with which she has received creative criticism has been an example to me of true humility. Joanne has shown herself approved and has given birth to a life-changing labor of love, for those who heed her words.

If your ministry involves relationships or marriage, whether you be male or female, this book is an essential tool. As most peoples' lives revolve around relationships of some kind, it makes for a great study book. I would also recommend it as a "couples" book, to be read and discussed together. You will no doubt go through emotional testings as "man-made" traditions are threatened, and maybe the challenges will hurt, but read on. Give this woman of God the honor of hearing her out to the end. If you will, I believe you will receive fresh revelation and bring joy to your lives and to those that love you.

We are both enthusiastic, for Graham and I, in our early walk with the Lord, went through most of the misconceptions and the traditional attitudes toward Christian women and marriage. Man — the head, the boss, the priest, and the decider. We became involved with a well-intentioned group that built up the male by putting the wife in a sub-servient position. The male was supreme; the female his obedient chattel.

Through much study of the Word, Graham and I began to understand this was not God's original intent for His children. We discovered through many tears, prayers, and frustrations this very message that Joanne has written in her book. We have made this subject our own lifestyle, living it for the past fifteen years. The outcome? A happy and deeply-in-love married couple, with mutual respect. We both believe this book is long overdue.

May your marriage and relationships be as God intended, and mercy, peace, and love be yours as you read.

Treena J. Kerr

International Bible Teacher
Producer of The Galloping Gourmet *and* The Graham Kerr
   Show

Word of Endorsement

I can heartily endorse the conclusions of Joanne's book. She has done an excellent job. Her book is biblically and theologically sound. It is easy to read and understand. She has included insights on Genesis, chapters 1-3; 1 Corinthians 11 and 14; and 1 Timothy 2, which I have not seen in a number of other books I have read on the subject.

Although I don't know specifically where they came from, my early convictions were that the husband was the boss in the home, and women had a limited role in the church. In 1976 I found myself having problems receiving from women in leadership in Youth with a Mission, the mission agency with which we were affiliated. Loren and Darlene Cunningham, leaders of YWAM, counseled with me and prayed for me regarding this. Their prayer included that God would use me to release women.

In 1981, while pastoring in Oregon, we were again confronted with this whole subject. As I continued to study and pray, God continued to change my views and open my heart to women. And He allowed me to begin releasing women into ministry. The years since then have been challenging years as I have had to come to grips with the various conclusions which Joanne has been reaching in her study and writing. It has not been easy to turn my back on a tradition which I had been led to believe was so biblical.

I can honestly say, however, understanding who women are in God's sight and His plan for them has greatly enhanced my regard for women in general, and my love and respect for my wife in particular. It has brought a dimension of mutual respect and trust to our marriage that was not present before. I no longer see

Joanne as someone given to me by God to help me in my ministry, but that we have been given to each other in order that together we might exalt His Name (Psalm 34:3).

I trust that God will use this book to influence millions of men and women around the world. I pray that husbands and church leaders will release women to become all that God wants to make them as godly partners in the home, church, and society.

Nate Krupp

Henceforth it is also war by Satan upon the womanhood of the world, in malignant revenge for the verdict of the garden. War by the trampling down of women in all lands where the deceiver reigns. War upon women in Christian lands, by the continuance of his Eden method of misinterpreting the Word of God; insinuating into men's minds throughout all succeeding ages, that God pronounced a "curse" upon the woman, when in truth she was pardoned and blessed; and instigating men of the fallen race to carry out the supposed curse, which was in truth a curse upon the deceiver, and not the deceived one (Genesis 3:14).

"I will put enmity between thee and the woman," said God, as well as between "thy seed and her seed," and this vindictive enmity of the hierarchy of evil to woman, and to believers, has not lessened in its intensity from that day.

— Jesse Penn-Lewis

Contents

Introduction

In 1988 my husband Nate and I found ourselves in a church situation where, we soon learned, women were not free to teach or even participate in the discussion of the Scriptures in any church meetings. Having been in a similar situation nearly twenty years earlier, my first reaction was, "Lord, not again! Please!" In the first situation, Nate had been in full agreement, but in the ensuing years, God had worked in his heart and understanding regarding women in ministry. He had brought him to the place where, as a spiritual leader, he was able to release women (including me) into whatever God called them to do. But, here we were again. How were we to respond to this situation?

Right at that time, Katherine Bushnell's book *God's Word to Women* came into Nate's possession. This book deals in-depth with the whole subject of the role of women from a biblical perspective. As he began reading it, the Holy Spirit prompted him that I, not he, should be reading the book. He gave it to me and as I began reading, I realized that I really did not know, in fact, had never studied the Scriptures for myself in order to learn what exactly God's plan for woman was. It was then that the Lord ignited within me an insatiable desire to delve into the subject and find the truth from God's Word.

I, like most of us, had been brought up with the traditional teaching regarding women that goes something like this: Eve, because she partook of the fruit of the forbidden tree first, was the cause of sin coming into the world. Because of her sin, a curse was placed upon her by God that was to include physical pain as her body would be involved in the reproductive process. She was also told by God that man was to rule over her. Although it had not been part of my early understanding, as I moved into adulthood, I learned that there were those who understood that, furthermore, the Scriptures teach that women are not to be involved in teaching the Word of God to men or hold any position of spiritual leadership.

As I studied, there was a question that loomed in my mind: "Was the premise for that traditional teaching found in the Bible, or brought to it by interpretation?"

I experienced many emotions as I studied. I experienced excitement as I came to understand who I am, as a woman, in God's sight. I experienced anger as I was faced with the way Scripture has been twisted to serve the purposes of male authoritarianism. I experienced grief as I pondered the degradation, oppression, and humiliation my sisters have needlessly suffered for centuries. But I also experienced joy as I came to see that God is in the process of restoring woman to her rightful position in society in general, and particularly in her relationship to her husband (and he to her), and her rightful place in the Church.

It is my desire to lead you on a pilgrimage through the Bible that will open the window of truth as it relates to God's plan for women. It is my prayer that this truth, when breathed in by the reader, will aid in healing the tremendous breach that exists between men and women in the Body of Christ.

This is by no means an exhaustive study on this subject. However, I hope I have included enough exegesis to show forth truth, but not so much that the reader might become "bogged down" with details.

Let me say at this point, I am not a feminist! Today, contrary to the purer definition of a century ago, the word "feminist" stands for the Equal Rights Amendment, abortion rights, and lesbianism. I want no part of any of these! I am even uncomfortable with the term, biblical feminist. That rather falls into the category of an oxymoron. Neither am I attempting to champion "women's rights." A truly broken Christian who has been crucified with Christ has no rights. Nor am I joining the ranks of those females who are fighting for recognition and superiority of lordship or rulership.

Rather, I am pressing for the God-given equality of submission and servanthood. I simply desire to see God's plan, as outlined in Scripture, lived out in the lives of believers. I long to see men and women, in the home, in the Church, and in all of society, functioning and relating to one another in the way God had in mind from the very beginning.

It is my prayer that this book will be used by God to hasten the day when that will be a reality.

ONE

In the
Beginning

*I*n order to get an accurate understanding of the kind of relationship God had in mind between man and woman, we must go back to the beginning, as recorded in Genesis. Genesis 1:26-28 gives a clear picture of the relationship that existed in the Garden of Eden; and therefore, gives a clear picture of what God's plan was for the type of relationship that should exist between a husband and wife.

The New American Standard translation says it this way:

> "Let Us make man in Our image, according to Our likeness; and let them rule over the fish of the sea and over the birds of the sky and over the cattle and over all the earth, and over every creeping thing that creeps on the earth." And God created man in His own image, in the image of God He created him; male and female He created them. And God blessed them; and

> God said to them, "Be fruitful and multiply, and fill the earth and subdue it; and rule over the fish of the sea and over the birds of the sky, and over every living thing that moves on the earth."

Together they were created in the image of God. Together they were to rule over the fish in the sea, over the birds in the sky, over the cattle, and over all the earth. God blessed them and told them to be fruitful, multiply, fill the earth, and subdue it. Both were to move through life on an equal status. Not one word is mentioned in this Scripture about man ruling over woman, or any other hierarchical authority arrangement, other than God Himself being over both of them.

Adam and Eve had a mutual, loving relationship in which they moved through that beautiful Garden as one flesh, according to Genesis 2:24:

> For this cause a man shall leave his father and his mother, and shall cleave to his wife; and they shall become one flesh.

Because sin had not yet entered the world, there was no vying for leadership, no competition, no claiming of rights, no jealousy, no shirking of responsibility (with one possible exception, i.e., when Adam didn't protect the Garden as God had instructed him, which we'll touch on later). They were just "one flesh" moving in unity.

Helper, Helpmeet, or What?

Now we know they each had their own unique contribution to make to their relationship. The Bible says God saw that it was not good for man to be alone, therefore He provided *"a helper suitable for him"* (Genesis 2:18). Apparently, Eve contributed something to Adam that he was lacking.

Let's look at the word "helper." *Ezer*, the Hebrew word for "help" in the Old Testament usage does not imply an inferior or subordinate help, but means "to help one in trouble." For example, Psalm 121:2 says, *"My help comes from the Lord."* Exodus 18:4 says, *"The God of my father was my help and delivered me from the sword of Pharoah."* Psalm 20:2 says, *"May He send you help from the sanctuary."* So it appears that the kind of help God saw that Adam needed, and that He created in the form of Eve, was a surrounding, defending, and undergirding help. This was a spiritual and emotional kind of help, not a "bring me my pipe and slippers" subordinate.

The King James Version (hereafter referred to as KJV) says "help meet;" NASB says "helper suitable." The Hebrew word *kenegdo*, translated "suitable," means "as his counterpart, those things which are like one another as a mirror reflection, corresponding to him." Therefore God was saying He was going to create someone for Adam who would be just like him. She would, however, add a dimension which Adam alone lacked; as a couple, then, they would be more complete. She was not to be considered his inferior or his subordinate; she would be just like him. Together they were created in God's image.

R. David Freedman defines *ezer* as more accurately meaning "power" (or strength) rather than "helper," since it is thus used elsewhere in the Hebrew Bible. Furthermore, based on Mishnaic Hebrew, he puts forth that *kenegdo*, usually rendered "suitable for him," actually means "equal to him." Therefore, when God said He would make a "helper suitable for him," He was saying that this woman would be a "power" equal to man, his match, corresponding to him in every way.[1]

Imagine the beautiful union — the smooth flowing together, the give-and-take, the oneness, because they were one flesh — that took place there in the Garden.

The sad part of that beautiful story is that it came to an end with the Fall. The intimate relationship Adam and Eve had with God and each other was broken and destroyed, altering the course of life for both man and woman ever since.

However, Jesus, with His death on the Cross and resurrection, has made possible the restoration of all things (Acts 3:21). Jesus' death and resurrection, as commonly understood, made possible: our being made new in Christ, a relationship with Him, a walk through life with knowledge of sins forgiven, and the hope of heaven. Beyond this, it also made possible the full restoration of all relationships on every level in this life (Ephesians 2:11-22).

Most importantly, it made possible the restoration of the kind of relationship between a husband and wife that existed before the Fall. Therefore, it is possible, under the Lordship of Jesus Christ and the power and anointing of the Holy Spirit, for a husband and wife to walk together through life with total unity, love, and equality. To say that this restoration does not include the restoration of that equal relationship between husband and wife, as experienced in the garden, is selling the Cross of Jesus Christ short and denying the power of His shed blood. Who are we to so restrict the complete work of Christ on the Cross?!

The Rib Origin

Let's take a look at the word "rib" as spoken of in Genesis 2:21, 22. The Hebrew word *tsela* is used fifty-two times in the Old Testament. These two verses are the **only** two verses where this word is translated "rib." In every other case it is translated either "side," "side-chamber," "chamber," or "corner." Had Eve been formed simply of Adam's rib, Adam would not have said, *"Bone of my bone* *and flesh of my flesh"* (Genesis 2:23), only "Bone of my bone."

The rib origin came from rabbinical lore which supports woman's low estate. Katherine Bushnell, in her book *God's Word to Women,* writes of a certain Rabbi Joshua who included this piece of lore in his commentaries, and it has been picked up by a number of Christian commentators on the Bible. Here is one rendition:

> God deliberated from what member He would create woman, and He reasoned with Himself thus: "I must not create her from Adam's head, for she would be a proud person, and hold her head high. If I create her from the eye, then she will wish to pry into all things; if from the ear, she will wish to hear all things; if from the mouth, she will talk much; if from the heart, she will envy people; if from the hand, she will desire to take all things; if from the feet, she will be a gadabout. Therefore, I will create her from the member which is hid, that is, the rib, which is not even seen when man is naked."[2]

A variation with which I grew up renders a more tender attitude. It concludes with, "I will create her from the rib, that part of the man's body that is closest to his heart." This lore, which has no scriptural basis, seems to accept Eve as something of an afterthought.

On the contrary, Genesis 5:1, 2 says:

> This is the book of the generations of Adam. In the day when God created man, He made him in the likeness of God. He created them **male** and **female**, and He blessed them and named **them** Man in the day when they were created. *(Bold added for emphasis.)*

I believe when God created Adam, He included something that would become the basis from which Eve would later be formed. She was not an after-thought.

When God caused the deep sleep to fall upon Adam, He simply lifted that "side" of Adam out, placed it in a female body, and presented her to Adam. She was now a corresponding, suitable, mirror-like reflection of Adam, created in the image of God from the very beginning. There is little comparison between this Eve and the one tradition has told us was formed by taking one little bone and creating a whole new being.

The Septuagint

It is important to note that the Septuagint version of the Old Testament translated these verses "side" rather than "rib."

The Septuagint version is one of the most important documents that we have as a reference on this or any other biblical subject. This translation from the Hebrew to the Greek was produced by seventy-two Jewish scholars in 285 B.C. Many consider it the most important of all versions. It is among the most ancient manuscripts and was translated at a time when more was known about the ancient Hebrew than at anytime since.

The Septuagint was much in favor among the Jews until Christians began using it to prove that Jesus was the Messiah. From that time it began to fall under Jewish displeasure. This is the text that was very probably used by the Lord Himself as well as the Apostles.[3] As Jesus read the Old Testament in the synagogue and taught against the traditions that had been handed down which nullified the Word of God (Mark 7:13), it is never recorded that He took exception to this translation, or any part of it.

The importance of the Septuagint translation must not be undermined. As we proceed in this discourse, other references will be made to its translation of certain important portions.

Conclusion

Based on this analysis of the creation story, one must conclude that the original plan God had in mind when He created man and woman was for unity, mutual support, and submission to each other – not for the subjugation of one over the other. I have come to agree with Faith Martin who has made the following statement in her book *Call Me Blessed:*

> A woman is an adult female human and, by reason of the honor and position granted her by God at Creation, stands beside the adult male human as his equal in all concerns of life.[4]

I am convinced that there is too much in Scripture supporting this statement for anyone to put and keep women in a lesser position. Nor did God change that through anything He said to Eve after the Fall. Let's return to the Garden and consider what really happened.

Chapter One Notes

1. R. David Freedman as quoted in Marvin R. Wilson, *Our Father Abraham* (Grand Rapids: Wm. B. Eerdmans Publishing Co. and Center for Judaic-Christian Studies, 1989), 201.

2. Katherine C. Bushnell, *God's Word to Women* (privately reprinted by Ray B. Munson, P.O. Box 417, North Collins, NY, 1923), 43.

3. Ibid., 130.

For further reference: Merrill F. Unger, *Unger's Bible Dictionary* (Chicago: Moody Press, 1957), 1147-49.

4. Faith Martin, *Call Me Blessed* (Grand Rapids: Wm. B. Eerdmans, 1988), 12.

TWO

What Really Happened in the Garden?

Satan Entered

*L*et's go back to the Garden scene and anaylze exactly what happened. Genesis 2:15 tells us, *"Then the Lord God took the man and put him into the garden of Eden to cultivate it and keep it."* According to *Gesenius' Hebrew-Chaldee Lexicon to the Old Testament*, "keep" means "to keep, to watch, to guard."[1]

I have this nagging question in the back of my mind: if Adam was guarding the Garden as God had instructed him, how did Satan get in there in the first place? It appears to me that Satan was the only thing from which the Garden needed protection. This was a responsibility given to Adam alone, since Eve had not yet been formed.

We know, of course, that Satan did enter the Garden and tempt Eve. She responded to that temptation, partook of the fruit, and gave to her husband who also ate of it. I used to think that Eve was all alone when temptation came to her and that when she partook of the fruit, eager to share it with Adam, she ran all over the Garden looking for him. Not so! Genesis 3:6 says, *"And she gave also to her husband with her and he ate."* He was there all along! Yet Scripture does not indicate he said anything to keep her from eating or to correct her deception.

Thus the Fall took place. A careful analysis of the scenario that followed between God and Adam and Eve is very important for one who desires to know whether the traditional teaching is fact or fiction. Let's follow it.

Beginning with Genesis 3:9, both Adam and Eve partook of the forbidden fruit. Then God came to deal with them. First, God asked Adam, *"Hast thou eaten of the tree?"* Some would say the fact that God went to Adam first indicates the role of authority Adam held. I believe the reason God went to Adam first was because the prohibition had been given to Adam before Eve had been taken out of man and placed in her own body. Therefore, Adam was in the place of full accountability to God.

Anytime God (or anyone else for that matter) gives you something to do or commands you not to do something, He is going to hold you accountable to His directions, not your spouse. If God told me to make restitution to a certain person and I failed to do it, God would not go to my husband and ask him whether I had obeyed. He would come to me, the one to whom He had given the directive, and ask, "Joanne, did you do what I asked you to do?" And if not, "Why?"

When God asked Adam, *"Hast thou eaten of the tree?,"* Adam replied, *"The woman whom Thou gavest to be with me, she gave me of the tree, and I did eat."* Then God questioned Eve. Her reply was, *"The serpent beguiled me and I did eat."*

Notice the difference in their replies. Eve blamed Satan. Adam blamed Eve, and ultimately, God. Adam made an evil choice. He blamed God and in so doing, moved to the side of Satan. Eve, on the other hand, fully exposed the character of Satan before his very face. By so doing, she caused Satan to hate her, and all woman-kind that followed her, with intense hatred.

Since that moment, Satan has done everything he could to put and keep woman down — and quite successfully. He also knew, however, from the very beginning how God had created woman as the counter-part (mirror-type, equal to) to Adam, and that God's plan at Calvary was to totally redeem woman back to her original position.

From the moment of Jesus' conception, the position of women began to be restored; and with each new reviving move of the Spirit from the Acts of the Apostles to the present, God has again and again called His daughters forth. Where the Spirit is there is liberty; and in the initial years of each revival, women have begun to rise to their God-given position. However, Satan, in turn, has launched new attacks to bring women down again.

Satan's Counterfeit

By the 1960s, even though equality existed in some parts of the Church, it was sadly lacking in others. At the beginning of what has come to be known as the Charismatic Renewal in the mid-60s, there began a new thrust by the Holy Spirit to lead women forward to their position of equality with man before God. This time, Satan raised up a counterfeit movement labeled the Women's Liberation Movement. This movement pushed the issue beyond equality of the sexes to a dominant role for the female, and acceptance of unnatural, ungodly male and female roles. This movement rose to its height in the 1970s and angrily continues to this day. I believe Satan instigated this movement, not because he wanted to see women liberated, but rather as a method to further divide the Church and alienate women and men. This has caused even more controversy toward women within the Body of Christ.

Sadly, the Church has not been able to recognize the enemy's tactics and separate this plan and its true source from God's genuine plan, as outlined in Scripture. The Feminist movement today continues to polarize the Church on the woman's issue causing a backlash towards women among those of traditional understanding. This is especially true among some fundamentalists and charismatics who hold to a strict understanding of male dominance.

Satan not only hates the woman for these reasons, but he knows all too well the power the Church will have when women, with men, take their God-ordained positions to stand in unity as one in Christ. Satan has, therefore, continued to do all he can to keep God's house divided. He has diminished its power by keeping half of the Body of Christ displaced, out of position, out of joint.

Consequently, much of the Body of Christ limps along, even at a time when we hear the Spirit echoing Jesus' prayer, *"Father, make them one;"* (John 17:21-23), and He continues to prepare Himself *"a glorious Church without spot or wrinkle or any such thing"* (Ephesians 5:27).

Between the counterfeit women's movement and the traditional position, we find our energies used up fighting each other rather than Satan. Oh, that women would be allowed to take their position (along with men) in Christ so that the world might see a true reflection and demonstration of Him through His entire Body in the world today!

The Messiah Promised

Adam blamed God. Eve blamed Satan. Both, however, acknowledged their sin by saying *"I did eat."* One has to acknowledge that the heart-attitude of one who blames God for his own sin is different from the one whose heart-attitude puts the blame at the feet of Satan. There is no spirit of repentance in one who is still blaming God for his sin.

What follows next is that marvelous first Messianic promise in Genesis 3:15. God speaks to Satan and says,

> And I will put enmity between you and the woman, and between your seed and her seed; He shall bruise you on the head, and you shall bruise him on the heel.

This is the first prophecy of the coming Messiah, Jesus.

It is important to note here that Eve believed in the coming Messiah, and she acknowledged that belief by her statement in Genesis 4:1. When she had her first child, she said, *"I have gotten a man-child with the help of the Lord."* The word for Lord here means "Jehovah - the Coming One." So Eve really was the first to acknowledge faith in the promised Messiah.

In summary:
1. Eve sinned, laid the blame at Satan's feet, and yet acknowledged her sin.
2. She believed in the promise of the One who would conquer her enemy for her, as was prophesied in Genesis 3:15.
3. She even accepted that One by faith as indicated in Genesis 4:1.

It seems to be very clear that all of this could have counted to her for righteousness. Abraham believed and it was counted unto **him** for righteousness (Genesis 15:6),

why not Eve?   Jesus is the same yesterday, today, and
forever!

This does not make Eve superior to Adam, just
forgiven.   But because of this, she certainly does not
deserve the curse that tradition has told us she received
from the hand of God.

Sin Entered the World Through Adam

After the fourth chapter of Genesis, Eve is never
referred to again in the Old Testament.   Adam is
mentioned two times, once in Job 31:33, *"If I, like Adam,
covered my transgression by hiding my iniquity in my bosom,"*
and again in Hosea 6:7, *"They, like Adam transgressed the
covenant."*   Both of these references mention his
transgression.

In the New Testament, it is plainly stated that Adam's
conduct brought sin into the world:

- Romans 5:12, *"By one man sin entered into the world."*
- Romans 5:14, *"Nevertheless, death reigned from Adam to
  Moses, even over those who had not sinned in the likeness
  of Adam's offense, who is a type of Him who was to
  come."*
- 1 Corinthians 15:22, *"In Adam all die."*

Eve indicates, as recorded in Genesis 3:13, that the
serpent deceived her when he tempted her.   1 Timothy
2:14 states, *"Adam was not deceived – but the woman being
quite deceived fell into transgression."*   We don't know all that
transpired to allow this deception, but it is important to
understand that the word "deceive" means to fool
someone so completely that he accepts what is false as
truth.

This does not negate the sin, but it would seem that
there is an even greater measure of mercy shown to those
who sin out of deception.   Paul said, in 1 Timothy 1:13:

> ... even though I was formerly a blasphemer and a
> persecutor and a violent aggressor. And yet I was
> shown mercy, because I acted ignorantly in unbelief.

So even though tradition lays the blame for the Fall at
Eve's feet, Scripture very clearly says that Adam willfully
sinned; and that it was, in fact, through Adam that sin
entered into the world.

Again, this does not make Eve superior, but certainly
does not put her in line for the kind of curse that tradition
claims was placed on her by God. The traditional doctrine
concerning Eve has placed an inferior light upon woman's
stature in God's sight; and, thus, greatly curtailed her
spiritual activity. This has caused the entire Church of
Jesus Christ to suffer, having been deprived of the full
ministry of anointed women.

Did God Curse Eve?

One of the most controversial verses in the Bible
relating to this whole issue is Genesis 3:16:

> To the woman He said, "I will greatly multiply
> your pain in childbirth, in pain you shall bring forth
> children; yet your desire shall be for your husband,
> and he shall rule over you."

It is the pivotal verse upon which the whole
male/female relationship rests. Its accurate translation is
crucial to the entire subject.

Most modern translations inaccurately render Genesis
3:16. However, it has been traced in history to the time
when a calculated change was made in the translation of
certain words. This change gave man the authority over
woman as if ordained by God. Ancient manuscripts verify
this calculated error.

So what does Genesis 3:16 really say? Let's begin with the first phrase, *"To the woman he said 'I will greatly multiply your pain in childbirth'"* (KJV – *"Thy sorrow and conception"*).

The ancient Hebrew word in this verse lacks two letters which it needs in order to be translated "childbirth" or "conception." Without those two letters, the word becomes "sighing" instead.[2] The Septuagint has translated that phrase "A snare hath increased thy sorrow and thy sighing."[3] The snare is Satan. He was the source of sorrow introduced into the world. God did not multiply woman's pain. Satan increased her sorrow and sighing.

The next phrase, *"in pain you shall bring forth children;"* or as the New International Version more accurately translates it, *"in pain you will bring forth children;"* has been interpreted to mean that, because of God's judgment, the birth process would always be accompanied by pain. However, one must keep in mind that in the beginning bringing forth children was to have been a blessing (Genesis 1:28). So the grief or the pain does not lay alone in the birth process, but, also in the whole rearing and raising process. God, in using the word "will," was warning Eve that pain and sorrow would accompany bringing children to a place of maturity in a world full of evil.

I recently asked an obstetrician if he ever has patients who give birth painlessly. He said, "Not totally painlessly, but there are women who give birth easily." I also have a friend who has testified to having had two almost painless births. This confirmed my conviction that if God had decreed that a woman was to have great pain in childbirth, based on this verse, then there could be no exceptions. God's decrees have no exceptions.

The Bible does have many references to women in travail or painful labor leading up to their time of delivery.

And more times than not, most of us mothers can testify to having experienced that kind of pain. However, I do not believe this is due to a "curse" having been placed upon woman by God. Rather, as He warned, it is the result of sin in general and its accompanying pain and sorrows.

The translation of the last part of the verse, *"Yet your desire shall be for your husband, and he shall rule over you,"* seems to rest on two words: "desire," and whether the correct verb form is "will" or "shall."

Let's look at the verb form first. "Shall" is an imperative. "Will" is a simple future verb indicating a warning. Shall declares that something **must** be done. Will is simply a prediction of something in the future. This phrase is written in the subjunctive, or conditional, tense which never implies a sense of obligation in the Semitic languages. Since the "wills" and the "shalls" are supplied by the translator, the word to be used can be proven only by the context and the tense in which the context is written. All the ancient manuscripts render this word as a simple future – a warning, not an imperative.[4]

Now what about that word "desire"? The Hebrew word *teshuqua* has traditionally been rendered as "desire" and interpreted as meaning "appetite" or "lust" in the modern translations. The concept of sensual desire can be traced back to the teaching of the rabbis in the *Talmud*.

The *Talmud* contains regulations and traditions handed down orally from one generation to another. These teachings gradually became law and were accepted to be as authoritative as the five Old Testament books of the Law, referred to by the Jews as the *Torah*. In fact, by the time Jesus began his ministry, the *Talmud* had almost entirely replaced the commandments of the Old Testament. Included in the *Talmud* are the "Ten Curses of Eve." Within these "Curses," rather crude language was used by the rabbis to depict woman's sensual desires.

Some of those today who hold to the traditional understanding, still believe "desire" to be the strong sexual desire that woman will have for man. This is not born out in reality since, generally speaking, a man has a stronger sex drive than a woman. There are those, however, who believe it is referring to the desire or appetite woman would have to rule over man (rather than allowing man to rule over woman as they believe God intended).

Teshuqua is used three times in the Old Testament: Genesis 3:16, Genesis 4:7, and Song of Solomon 7:10. Genesis 3:16 and Genesis 4:7 have been translated into Greek in the Septuagint as the word *apostrophe*, meaning "turning away." Song of Solomon 7:10 has been translated into the Greek with the word *apistrophe* in the Septuagint, meaning "turning to." Again, referring to the Septuagint, this verb was translated "thou art turning away to thy husband and he will rule over thee." The meaning seems to imply that Eve would be turning away from God (this new-found relationship with God) toward her husband. Consequently, because of this defection, Adam would rule over her.

In his book *Hard Sayings of the Old Testament*, Walter Kaiser says,

> Of the twelve known ancient versions (the Greek Septuagint, the Syriac Peshitta, the Samaritan Pentateuch, the Old Latin, the Sahidic, the Bohairic, the Ethiopic, the Arabic, Aquila's Greek, Symmachus's Greek, Theodotion's Greek, and the Latin Vulgate), almost every one (twenty-one out of twenty-eight times) renders these three instances of *teshuquah* as "turning," not "desire."[5]

Kaiser goes on to say,

> Bushnell traced the change in translation to an Italian Dominican monk, Pagnino, who translated the

Hebrew Bible. His version was published in Lyons in
1528. Now, with the exception of Wycliff's 1380
English version and the Douay Bible of 1609, both of
which were made from the Latin Vulgate, every
English version from the time of Pagnino up to the
present day has adapted Pagnino's rendering for
Genesis 3:16.[6]

Thus, the modern day translation "desire" comes from
Pagnino's rendering, not from the ancient Hebrew.

A friend recently shared with me her experience which
bears this out. I was explaining this concept regarding the
accurate translation of the word *teshuqua*, turning away
from God to her husband. Her response was very
interesting.

She said,

> Joanne, you know, that is exactly what I did. When
> I was first converted, my only desire was to please
> God. Anything He told me to do, I did it. I had a very
> intimate relationship with Him. Then when my
> husband found the Lord, I turned to him and did
> everything I thought he wanted me to do, anything
> that would please him. Many times I did what I knew
> my husband wanted even when, in my spirit, I didn't
> have peace about a given situation. That is what I have
> been taught a good Christian wife should do. Now I
> see that in that turning, I forfeited a very precious and
> intimate relationship with the Lord in order to please
> my husband.

Based on this verse, it is part of the carnal nature of a
woman to please her husband. As in the case of my
friend, that carnal desire was broken at her conversion and
her desire then moved to that of pleasing the Lord. Now,
we all know that if she is pleasing the Lord she is going to
be a super wife to her husband which should bring him
much pleasure. When a believing husband is introduced
into this picture with the traditional "ruler husband"

teaching, the wife is basically taught to revert to the natural or carnal way of living. This way of living implies the view of "don't listen as closely to God as you listen to your husband. Give up that intimacy with God." What a travesty it is when women are either never allowed to develop this intimacy with God or when women are forced to forfeit it in order to "properly" submit to their husbands.

Having an intimate relationship with God, where listening intently to His voice and obeying His every command is important above all else, is the greatest gift a wife can give her husband and the most valuable contribution she can make to her marriage. If women would only understand this principle, what wives they would be! They would then be free to be that "helper suitable" that God intended them to be.

Of course, the ideal is for both husbands and wives to have that same kind of relationship with the Lord. This kind of marriage can't fail. These families won't fall apart. That kind of a relationship is as near to heaven on earth as is possible to experience.

Many Christians believe that:

1. God originally placed Adam over Eve.
2. The result of sin entering into the world through Adam destroyed Eve's natural, pure response to his authority.
3. Because of the Fall, Eve then "desired" to rule her husband.

Of these three, I believe Scripture confirms only that sin entered the world through Adam. However, even if they **all** were true, God still **never** would have placed on fallen man the responsibility of restoring his so-called "God-given" position of authority which was destroyed by the Fall. This would have established man as his own savior — humanism in its rankest form. God also would not have given that authority to an unregenerate man, as

Adam was. It would have been difficult enough for a regenerate man to have handled that kind of authority, as we have watched so many men try to do. Given to an unregenerate man, that command would surely have been abused, as time also has sadly proven.

God always gives His command directly to the one whose responsibility it is to carry it out. Remember, God was speaking to Eve in Genesis 3:16, not Adam. If man ruling over woman had been the edict pronounced by God at that time — a responsibility that Adam was to carry — God would have spoken this directly to Adam rather than to Eve.

If the Hebrew verb in Genesis 3:16 were a command rather than a warning, then the more forcefully a man domineered his wife, the more spiritual he would be. However, it seems that the closer a man walks with God, the more mature and secure he becomes, the more whole he is, and the less he seems to need or desire to rule his wife (or anyone else for that matter). The spiritually mature husbands I have observed openly honor and cherish their wives and release them completely from any sense of bondage to their husbands.

Although God's plan for husbands and wives was mutual submission, He warned Eve that, as a result of the Fall, the natural (carnal) instinct of man would be to rule over her. He also warned her that her turning away from God to her husband would make that "ruling" a greater temptation. I believe man's carnal instinct to rule over woman has caused the erroneous translation of Genesis 3:16. This, in turn, has perpetrated the traditional teaching and practice.

We will look next at how God did, in fact, use women in leadership both in the Old and the New Testament, during the centuries when women experienced extreme suppression from the hands of men.

Chapter Two Notes

1. *Gesenius' Hebrew and Chaldee Lexicon to the Old Testament* (Grand Rapids: Baker Book House, 1981), ref. 8104.

2. Walter Kaizer, *Hard Sayings of the Old Testament* (Downers Grove, IL: InterVarsity Press, 1988), 31-32.

3. Katherine C. Bushnell, *God's Word to Women* (privately reprinted by Ray B. Munson, P.O. Box 417, North Collins, NY, 1923), 121.

4. Ibid., 127.

5. Kaizer, op. cit., 34.

6. Ibid., 34.

THREE

Women in the
Old Testament

As Men Began to Rule

*W*hat did life hold for women after the Fall and throughout the Old Testament? As we proceed, we'll see to what extent women were generally held in low esteem. At the same time we will observe how God raised up certain women to places of leadership and blessed them.

It's important to recognize the blessing of God upon these women. Scripture records many things that were not part of God's plan. When, however, we can read His pronouncement of blessing upon someone we can know that their actions were inspired of God.

As we discussed in Chapter Two, God warned Eve that man would rule over her. This "ruling" first became apparent with a man by the name of Lamech. Genesis 4:19

says that Lamech "took" for himself two wives. This is the
first evidence of polygamy and the first indication that
God's intended plan for marriage had been reversed.

Lamech's "taking" of a wife is in direct opposition to
the first scriptural law of society and marriage. In Genesis
2:24 God said,

> For this cause a man shall leave his father and his
> mother, and shall cleave to his wife, and they shall
> become one flesh.

This is not some archaic law that was mentioned once
way back in the beginning of the Bible never to be heard
again. On the contrary, this verse is quoted a total of four
times in the Bible. First, by God the Father in Genesis 2:24;
then God the Son in Matthew 19:5 and Mark 10:7; and
finally by God the Holy Spirit through Paul in Ephesians
5:31. Obviously there was a very important point God
was wanting to make, as all three in the Godhead stated it.

I believe God was setting down guidelines which
indicated first to Adam, at the time Eve was formed, the
extent to which he was to give himself to his wife to love
her, cherish her, and nourish her. And in order to give
himself to her to that degree he had to "cleave" to her,
attach himself to her in such a way that they would
become one flesh. For succeeding generations, this would
require that a man leave that which he had previously
"clung" to, namely his father and mother.

For the most part, in earliest human history, it would
appear that this law was acted upon.[1] It was customary
for the husband to leave his family and either live under
the roof of his wife's parents or live in close proximity and
make frequent visits. This gave the parents of the wife the
opportunity to "eye" this man to see if he was properly
caring for their daughter. The mother and father of a
daughter are her natural protectors, totally different from
the mother and father of a son.

I personally found this to be true. Let me relate to you my own journey. I have a son, Gerry, and a daughter, Beth, both of whom I absolutely adore. Yet, as adults, my mother's heart protects, surrounds, and goes out to Beth in a different way than it does to Gerry. When Gerry was young and approaching his courting and marrying age, I really did not know if there was any woman alive worthy of him. Somehow, I didn't worry about Beth in the same way. As I pondered the difference in my feelings regarding them, I concluded that there was a built-in sense that when Gerry left, I would be transferring his care over to his wife. I knew he would be "leaving" my care in order to "cleave" to his wife. I knew this was "right" but I wasn't sure there was a woman alive to whom I could entrust this precious son of mine.

It didn't take long for us to fall in love with Wenda after we met her, so as their wedding approached, we were truly at peace regarding this union. Any remaining fears were allayed the last time he was home before his wedding with what might appear to be a very insignificant detail.

I had cut Gerry's hair from the time he was a toddler until he went away to college where he met his future wife. After he and Wenda began going together, she began cutting his hair. As it turned out, he needed a haircut while he was at home this time so out came our clippers, and I went to work. As I was nearing the completion of the job, Gerry very matter-of-factly informed me that he liked Wenda's haircuts better than mine. (Mine weren't that bad, but without question, Wenda's had a finesse about them that mine lacked.) When he said that, something inside me just welled up with joy. Not only was I turning my son over to a woman who could possibly do as good a job taking care of him as I, but she was, in actuality, going to do a better job.

So it was with great joy that Nate and I were able to give our blessing to their marriage. Our love for Gerry has not decreased one iota, neither has his love and respect lessened toward us. But the "leaving" and "cleaving" has definitely taken place.

With Beth, there was a built-in sense that my care and concern for her would always be needed. Granted, it took on a different form as we joyfully released her to be joined in marriage with her wonderful husband Greg and allowed them the freedom to establish their own family. Even though we live close to them geographically now, that has not always been the case, but the natural desire to protect her has and always will be there.

The extended family in one locality can be of immeasurable blessing to the grandchildren growing up, even when the immediate family unit is strong. The older generation adds a dimension of wisdom and security to the younger generations.

In this mobile world that we live in, where parents and children alike are constantly moving around, the logistical reality of this concept is almost non-existent. We all know of situations among believers today where it is the wife who has left her home to go with her husband and the outcome has been joyously blessed by God. But is there Scripture to support this? I believe there is.

In Genesis 24, when Abraham's servant went back to Abraham's family to find a wife for Isaac, Rebecca was given the choice as to whether or not she wanted to go. She was not forcibly "taken" or coerced into going. But she chose to go – with God's blessing.

In the New Testament, it would appear, based on 1 Corinthians 9:5, that someone had brought a wife along on that missionary journey. It would be assumed that she had been led by the Holy Spirit to accompany her husband. Also in Acts 18, Aquila and Priscilla relocated twice. They were first forced to leave Italy because they were Jews. Then they went to Ephesus with Paul for the sake of the Gospel. They were simply living out Jesus' command in Mark 16:15 to *"Go into all the world and preach the gospel to all creation."* Many of us have been led of the Lord to relocate, leaving parents and family in order to fulfill His call on our lives.

But for the wife to leave her parents in order to, with her husband, follow the will of the Lord for their lives is far different from the "taking" of a wife as Lamech did. So what should be the reality of the "leaving" and "cleaving" command of the Lord in our lives today?

This "leaving" and "cleaving" must become a reality in the heart of a husband whether or not he ever leaves the locality where his parents reside. When a young man marries a wife, he must determine in his heart that he is going to devote his life to loving and cherishing her above all other humans, including his mother and father. We sometimes jokingly refer to this as "cutting the apron strings," but it really is no laughing matter. It is a very serious step that a man must take.

We know that the custom had been reversed by the time of the New Testament. When Christ was on earth, it was customary for the groom to go to the bride's home, fetch her, and take her to his father's house. Jesus' parable of the ten virgins, however, tells no such story. Jesus never violated the laws of God. When the bridegroom arrived at the home of the bride, he went in and the door was shut. There is no mention of his "taking" the bride away.

When Lamech "took" wives, he began the reversal of God's original plan. Wickedness prevailed, and then came the flood.

After the flood came the story of Abraham and the beginning of the Hebrew nation. Some have asked, "Why did God establish the patriarchal system (through Abraham, Isaac, and Jacob) if man was not to rule?" God didn't establish the patriarchal system. Ancient

civilizations had been ruled by patriarchal systems for
generations. Women had been ruled over and subservient
to men since the Fall.[2]

When God began establishing the nation of Israel, He
was actually setting the stage — preparing a people — for
the coming of the Messiah Who would restore all things.
This included the lifting up of women to their God-given
status in life. Thus, He would do away with the
patriarchal system.

With the beginning of the nation of Israel, under the
patriarchs Abraham, Isaac, and Jacob, God began setting
boundaries. He began laying ground rules to move
society back to the place which He originally intended.
God always uses what He has, or what exists, to move
people to the next place He has for them. He starts with
people where they are and moves them onward.

Women's Low Estate in the Old Testament

To show just how far God had to bring society, let's
look at some examples that portray the less-than-second-
class citizenship experienced by women in the Old
Testament.

Genesis 12:10-20 and 20:1-13 are two examples
involving Abraham and Sarah where Abraham told Sarah
to say she was his sister. In so doing, Sarah made herself
vulnerable to be taken into other men's harems. Abraham
obviously was more concerned for his own safety than for
his wife's virtue.

Even in our society today only the most depraved of
men would set his wife up for such treatment. Yet,
Abraham, the one with whom God had made a covenant,
saw his wife not as one to be loved and cherished, but as
one to be used that he might be spared.

Genesis 19:1-8 gives a clear picture of the abhorrent status of women in that day. It relates the story of Lot and his willingness to give his own virgin daughters to the wicked men of Sodom in order to protect the male guests in his home.[3]

Judges 19-21 tells the story of a young girl who was so raped and abused by the Benjamites in the town of Gibeah that she died. As a result, the rest of the sons of Israel set out to avenge the girl. In the ensuing battle, it was feared that the tribe of Benjamin would be completely annihilated. Not wanting to see that happen, the rest of the sons of Israel devised a plan whereby the Benjamites could "kidnap" women to be their wives. This story shows not only the lack of respect for women, but portrays the utterly degraded state in which they existed.

God's Blessing on Women

However, as God revealed Himself to His people, a gradual change came over Hebrew society. Women began to be used and blessed by God in various ways and situations. Let's look at some examples, beginning with Sarah.

We have covered how Sarah suffered as a woman, but she had some positive experiences as well. Her name was taken from the Hebrew word *Sar* meaning "chieftainess." It would appear that she had her own independent residence at Hebron (Genesis 23:2) and lived there while Abraham lived at Beersheba (Genesis 22:19). Abraham went to Hebron when Sarah died to mourn for her and bury her.

> Her position, therefore, during her wanderings and
> in later life was not by any means that of secluded
> dependence, but rather that of an independent head of
> the tribe, or "tribal mother."[4]

Miriam, in Exodus 15:20, is described as a prophetess. In Micah 6:4, God said, *"I sent before you Moses, Aaron, and Miriam."* God set Miriam as one of the leaders over Israel.

Numbers 27:1-11 is another example of how God was easing the Children of Israel into the acceptance and recognition of women. This is the story of the Daughters of Zelophehad who stood before Moses and all the people and requested possessions from among their father's brothers, since their own brothers were dead. Moses went to God Who said, "Give it to them." Furthermore, God said that from that day forth, if a man died with no sons, the inheritance was to be given to his daughters. This was a tremendous change in the whole life of the Hebrew nation. Up to this time, women were not allowed to own property. These women were extremely bold and brave to stand before Moses and say, "Hey, look, this isn't fair. We don't have any male to receive our inheritance. Why should we not receive what is rightfully ours?" God told Moses to honor their request, which changed the course of history.

Judges 4:4-23 tells of Deborah, a prophetess, who was one of several judges of Israel whom God raised up to lead His wayward people back to Him and against their enemies. God chose to use Deborah to lead and encourage the Children of Israel in the battle against Jabin, King of Canaan. She gave Barak the "word of the Lord" concerning the battle. Barak was willing to do as Deborah said, but only if she would accompany them to battle. God honored His word and delivered the Canaanites into their hands. This included Sisera, the commander of Jabin's army, who was killed by a woman Jael. The battle was won; victory was theirs; and in Judges 5 we have the lovely, victorious song that is sung by Deborah and Barak. Her words are recorded in the Scriptures, the significance of which we'll touch on later. Israel was desolate until Deborah arose, a "Mother in Israel" (Judges 5:7).

Abigail, in 1 Samuel 25, is one who operated contrary to her husband Nabal's wishes. Upon hearing of David's request, without consulting her husband, Abigail took provisions to David and his men. She knew full well that Nabal had just refused to give David anything. I do not believe Abigail was operating out of a rebellious heart just for the sake of defying her husband. Her heart told her David's needs should be ministered to, and she was simply taking what she felt was the right course of action. God clearly honored her decision. He smote Nabal ten days later, and he died. The Word says Abigail was *"a woman of good understanding"* or *"intelligence"* (1 Samuel 25:3).

Huldah was a prophetess (2 Kings 22:8-20) sought out by the king's priest to inquire of the Lord concerning His Word for the king and the people. This course was taken, not because there was no male prophet available at this time, for both Jeremiah (Jeremiah 1:1, 2) and Zephaniah (Zephaniah 1:1) were her contemporaries. This resulted in tremendous reform by Josiah the king including the celebration of the Passover which had not taken place for many years. It was a real revival! Huldah is an excellent example of a woman giving a man (the king) "the word of the Lord."

Hannah made a vow to the Lord without consulting her husband (1 Samuel 1:9-23). Eli the priest blessed her, and Elkanah her husband obviously agreed with her. This vow resulted in their first-born Samuel being taken to the temple at a very early age to be raised by the priest and to serve God. Not a small vow to make.

The traditional teaching regarding women in ministry discourages or even prohibits women from being in spiritual leadership. The Word of God is our guide for truth. Truth has no exceptions. Truth is unchangeable. Only one example is needed of a woman who ruled or exercised authority or initiative, without being granted

permission by her male guardian, and was clearly blessed
by God for doing so, to undermine this traditional
teaching. We have cited not one but four such examples in
the Old Testament: Deborah, Abigail, Huldah, and
Hannah. The New Testament contains examples as well
which we will examine in Chapter 10.

Important Old Testament Scriptures

There are several Scriptures in the Old Testament
which can not be overlooked as it relates to the role
women are to play in the Kingdom of God.

Psalm 68:11 – *"The Lord gives the command (Word).
Great is the company of women who proclaim it"* (KJV). NASB
says, *"the women who proclaim the good tidings are a great
host."*

One can not silence the half of the human race to
whom God has given the command to "proclaim."

Joel 2:28, 29 tells us:

> And it will come about after this that I will pour
> out My Spirit on all mankind; and your sons and
> daughters will prophesy, your old men will dream
> dreams, your young men will see visions. And even
> on the male and female servants I will pour out My
> Spirit in those days.

This is Joel's prophecy to Judah which is later quoted
by Peter on the day of Pentecost (Acts 2:16-18). It is a clear
indication that the Holy Spirit was to be poured out upon
women as well as men. The significance of this will be
dealt with in Chapter 10.

Jeremiah 9:17, 18, 20 says,

> Thus says the Lord of hosts, "Consider and call for
> the mourning women, that they may come; and send
> for the wailing women, that they may come!" (vs. 17).

"And let them make haste, and take up a wailing for us, that our eyes may shed tears, and our eye lids flow with water" (vs. 18).

Now hear the word of the Lord, O you women, and let your ear receive the word of His mouth; teach your daughters wailing, and every one her neighbor a dirge (vs. 20).

Today's counterpart to the "wailing" or "mourning" woman in the Old Testament is the intercessor. The Lord's call for the "wailing women" is a distinct call of God upon women for intercession. We are seeing this call of God being answered today as never before. Great numbers of women all over the world are responding to the call to give themselves to the ministry of intercession.

I believe the one who attempts to silence or control the ministry of women is on dangerous ground. As we have just seen, God used women in the Old Testament in powerful ways as they acted totally independent of men, yet with His blessing.

Now let's see what we find in the New Testament.

Chapter Three Notes

1. For further discussion on female kinship including numerous ancient historical examples, see Katherine C. Bushnell, *God's Word to Women* (privately reprinted by Ray B. Munson, P.O. Box 417, North Collins, NY, 1923), 415-464.

2. Faith Martin, *Call Me Blessed* (Grand Rapids: Wm. B. Eerdmans Publishing Co., 1988), 34.

3. We know that these guests were angels, vs. 1, but they came in the appearance of men and were referred to as men in vss. 5, 8, 10, 12, and 16.

4. Bushnell, op. cit., 59.

FOUR

Jesus' Attitude Toward Women

*I*n *His Steps* by Charles Shelton, written a number of years ago and considered a classic, is centered around a group of people who pledged for one year to do nothing without first asking, "What would Jesus do in this situation?" As those who made this commitment followed through, lives were changed, relationships were healed, peace reigned. If Christians would follow Jesus' example and respond to women as He did, I'm convinced the atmosphere in the Church would be different today.

Let's take a look at the Gospels and see what Jesus did in relation to women. How did He respond and relate to women while He was on earth? There is much to be learned simply by observing His actions and responses toward women in light of Jewish laws and traditions of that day.

Even the way the news of the coming of the Messiah
was delivered to Mary is in direct opposition to the
tráditional viewpoint as it relates to the husband being "in
charge." If such rulership had been ordained of God from
the beginning, Mary would not have been the first to learn
of the coming "blessed event." God would have sent the
message through Joseph because, as her betrothed, he
would have been over her in the line of authority.
However, to the contrary, the angel appeared to Mary first
(Luke 1:26-38), and she agreed to be the mother of the
Messiah without even consulting her husband. Joseph
knew nothing about it until after the fact (Matthew 1:18-
25). It was only when he wanted *"to put her away"* (vs. 19)
that the angel appeared to him and clued him in on what
was happening.

As we look into the Scriptures and discover how Jesus
and women interacted, we need to remember that
according to the Babylonian *Talmud*:

1. Women were considered mere chattel,
   and the possessions of men;
2. It was Jewish law that the woman's
   voice was not to be heard in public; and
3. She could not be used as a witness in
   any situation.[1]

When we examine specific scenarios involving Jesus
(or anyone else in the Bible for that matter), we must
remember many stories in the Bible include Eastern
customs that were (and are today) readily understood by
the Eastern mind. Unfortunately, few of us from Western
culture know much about them. Therefore some, if not
much, of the meaning behind a narrative or parable can be
lost to us. The Holy Spirit, in His faithfulness to "teach us
all things," reveals to us the overall spiritual truths; but I
wonder how many deep nuggets we have missed because
we lack knowledge about the customs that precipitated
various biblical situations.

Mary and Martha

For instance, in the story of Mary and Martha (Luke 10:38-42) the emphasis is usually placed on Martha's being so busy making preparations for Jesus and, no doubt, others who were traveling with Him, that she didn't have the time to sit at Jesus' feet and learn. The lesson projected then is that we should not get so busy with the mundane things of life that we don't have time to be with the Lord.

What is overlooked is that the Jewish oral law forbade the teaching of the law to Jewish women. They were not to sit at anyone's feet to be taught spiritual truths.[2] For Mary to have placed herself in this position was, to say the least, unusual. Jesus was attempting to put Mary at ease even as He spoke to Martha when He said, "*. . . Mary has chosen the good part, which shall not be taken away from her.*" This response was in direct opposition to the custom of the day, but Jesus was in the process of turning "customs" around to conform to God's plan for women. He came *"to set the captive free,"* and that included Mary.

Woman with the Issue of Blood

In Matthew 9:20-22 the story is told of the woman with the issue of blood. One needs to review Leviticus 15 to fully appreciate what Jesus did here. The children of Israel were taught the importance of cleanliness. Great detail was given as to how these procedures were to be carried out. Leviticus 15 specifically dealt with a woman who had an issue of blood. Anyone touching her, or anyone she touched, was made unclean until proper washings took place and time periods elapsed.

However, Jesus disregarded these laws when dealing with the woman in this story. Her faith told her that she only needed to touch Jesus' garment and she would be made whole. Upon doing so, did Jesus reprimand her and ask her why she was not following the Levitical law regarding uncleanness? Did he remind her that she should not even be mingling in a crowd of people? No! He healed her, called her "daughter," and acknowledged her faith.

Woman Bent Over by a Spirit

In Luke 13: 10-17, Jesus healed a woman bent over by a spirit. He singled her out, called her to come to Him, and healed her. Afterwards she glorified God. It would appear there was some audible manifestation of praise to the Lord contrary to the Jewish law of public silence for women. And Jesus called her a *"daughter of Abraham,"* a blessing the Lord Jesus gave because of her faith (Galatians 3:7). Jesus did not differentiate between her, a woman, and men referred to as *"sons of Abraham"* (Luke 19:9) because of their faith.

Woman Taken in Adultery

The woman taken in adultery in John 8:3-11 is a classic example of the depths to which society had gone in its prejudice against women. Again, one must compare this situation with the law that had been given in Leviticus 20:10. This law specifically said that both the adulterer and adulteress were to be put to death. Yet when the Scribes and Pharisees brought this woman caught in the act of adultery, they totally misquoted that law to Jesus. They said only that Moses commanded them to stone such women. Not one word was said about the adulterer. However, the Lord would have no part of their scheme. He placed the responsibility back upon them, and He forgave the woman. Finally someone had appeared on the scene to take the woman's side in this society of injustice.

The Samaritan Woman

The significance of Jesus' conversation with the woman at the well in John 4:3-42 is increased not only because he was conversing with a woman, but she was also a Samaritan with whom the Jews had had trouble, even bloodshed, for years. Not only did Jesus ask her, a Samaritan, for a drink of water, a practice that is acceptable as long as there is no further conversation, but he continued on, engaging her in the dialogue in which He revealed that He was the Messiah.

Jesus broke all the rules:

1.   Jews avoided Samaria if at all possible;
2.   He asked water of her, a Samaritan woman (even she was amazed, vs. 9); and
3.   He conversed with this woman, a totally unacceptable behavior for that day and situation.

The result of this conversation was that she became the first woman to bring men to Christ. She went back into the city to tell about this man who knew everything about her. Jesus was persuaded to stay there for two days and many believed on Him.

Mary Magdalene

A scene often overlooked in the New Testament is the one in the garden after Jesus' resurrection. To whom did He first appear after emerging from the grave? Mary! And what did He say to her? "Go, tell!" He commissioned her with the responsibility of telling His disciples the greatest story ever told — Jesus is risen (John 20:11-18)!

So Jesus proceeded to revolutionize a number of Jewish laws and traditions regarding women:

1. He encouraged a woman to learn about Him.
2. He spoke with women publicly. (A Jewish Rabbi would not even speak to his wife in public.)
3. He did not rebuke an unclean woman for touching Him.
4. He did not rebuke a woman who spoke in public (praising God).
5. He prevented the stoning of an adultress.
6. He conversed with a Samaritan woman.
7. He gave a commission to a woman — "Go, tell!"

Indeed, Jesus shocked all who observed His personal attention and appreciation toward women in every station of life. As Jesus walked on earth as the Son of Man, He became the first man to defend, uphold, and honor womanhood. His shocking behavior was continued by the apostle Paul.

Many say that there are New Testament Scriptures where Paul takes a chauvinistic stance regarding women, going so far as to silence them completely. Not so, as we will see.

Chapter Four Notes

1. Charles Trombley, *Who Said Women Can't Teach?* (North Brunswick, NJ: Bridge Publishing, 1985), 31.

2. Katherine C. Bushnell, *God's Word to Women* (privately reprinted by Ray B. Munson, P.O. Box 417, North Collins, NY, 1923), 202, 335, 610.

FIVE

Introduction to
Paul's Writings

*T*he apostle Paul is the one most often credited with giving directives regarding the subordinate role of women. However, I'm convinced Paul would never have made a statement which would have silenced a group of people whom God says are to proclaim the Word of God (Psalm 68:11), and whom God said in the last days would be anointed to prophesy (Joel 2:28, 29). Neither should spiritual leaders today assume that authority.

One can not take an isolated social issue, use a few proof texts and make them say what one wants them to say, disregarding all previous principles and moral imperatives that have already been laid down. Psalm 119:160 declares, *"The sum of Thy word is truth."* As it relates to our issue, all biblical teaching in the Old Testament, the Gospels, and the Acts of the Apostles tell of woman's place before and after the Fall. They show how God accepted, released, and anointed women, thereby reaffirming His plan for equality. To isolate and interpret Paul's writings for what they appear to be saying would negate all that the Scriptures have taught previously, which we simply do not have the liberty to do.

Throughout the Old Testament, the Gospels, and the Acts, not one word has been said about the authority role of husbands over wives — not one (keeping in mind the proper translation of Genesis 3:16).

To attribute to Paul the total reversal of the heretofore mentioned principles and moral imperatives laid down in the Bible is to undermine Paul's intelligence, spiritual acumen, and his credibility. Remember, Paul was a well-educated man, highly skilled in his knowledge of the Old Testament. Also, keep in mind, the Word of God, including Paul's writings, was inspired by the Holy Spirit and does not contradict itself.

However, one can not ignore 1 Corinthians 11, 1 Corinthians 14, Ephesians 5, and 1 Timothy 2. So what was Paul saying? There is a very adequate explanation and interpretation for each of these Scriptures which does not contradict the theology laid down in previous Scriptures. However, one must adhere to proper rules of interpretation.

Rules of Interpretation

There have been rules of interpretation accepted by biblical scholars for over two thousand years. Here is one form of those rules:

> 1. Rule of Definition - Define the term of words being considered and then adhere to the defined meanings.

2. Rule of Usage - Don't add meanings to established words and terms. What was the common usage in the cultural and time period when the passage was written?

3. Rule of Context - Avoid using words out of context. Context must define terms and how words are used.

4. Rule of Historical Background - Don't separate interpretation and historical investigation.

5. Rule of Logic - Be certain that words as interpreted agree with the overall premise.

6. Rule of Precedent - Use the known and commonly accepted meaning of words, not obscure meanings for which there is no precedent.

7. Rule of Unity - Even though many documents may be used there must be general unity among them.

8. Rule of Inference - Base conclusions on what is already known and proven or can be reasonably implied from known facts."[1]

What we have discussed so far is that man and woman had a perfect relationship of unity and equality in the Garden. After the Fall, because of sin, man had a desire to, and therefore did, rule over woman. We have seen this tendency to rule exemplified quite strongly in the Old Testament, yet we have also seen the number of situations where women were called by God to be leaders, and their leadership was blessed by God. We have seen situations where wives went against the will of their husbands or did things that might be considered to be undermining their husband's authority, yet were blessed by God.

The question raised is this: If God had desired to lay down the law of male authority for all time, would He ever have blessed something contrary to that principle? The answer is "No." Truth is truth, and there is no exception to truth. It would be totally contrary to the character of God to lay down a law and establish a pattern that He had intended to be carried out through all time and then to violate His own law by blessing someone who had operated in a contradictory manner.

Progression, not Regression

Another important aspect is the progression of Scripture, or the evolving of Scripture from the Old Testament to the New Testament. We move from the law of the Old Testament to the grace of the New. Indeed, from the bondage of the Old Testament to the freedom in Christ in the New. We are moving from the first Covenant which called for the blood of bulls and goats to the New Covenant where Christ's shed blood paid for our sin once and for all. This is the progression of the Bible, not regression. To move women from a state of freedom which included opportunity to exercise a leadership role in the Old Testament, to the bondage of the subservient role that many would have us believe the New Testament teaches, is simply not in keeping with the overall biblical pattern of progression.

Neither Male nor Female

Paul said in Galations 3:28, *"There is neither male* (and most translations say) *nor female."* This is an incorrect translation. It should read ". . . *there is neither Jew nor* (oude) *Greek, there is neither slave nor* (oude) *free man, there is neither male AND* (kai) *female."* Paul is saying Jew and Greek are opposites, bond and free are opposites, but concludes with male AND female. They are considered equals, not opposites, but a mirror-like reflection of each other.

Some traditionalists would say that Paul is referring here only to the fact that salvation is available to everyone no matter their lot in life. However, the word "salvation" means "wholeness," "completeness" in every area of life, and the means of the restoration of all things. This restoration must include the kind of relationship God ordained for man and woman in the Garden of Eden. Furthermore, this work of salvation does not stop with what Christ can do for women, but also includes what Christ can do through them by way of ministry. **Everything that is available to men who are "in Christ" is also available to women.** This is born out in the correct understanding of Paul's writings, which we will see in the following chapters.

Chapter Five Notes

1. Charles Trombley, *Who Said Women Can't Teach?* (North Brunswick, NJ: Bridge Publishing, 1985), 135-36.

SIX

What About
Submission and
Headship?

Ephesians 5:21-33

*O*ne of the most important and misunderstood New Testament passages dealing with husbands and wives is Ephesians 5:21-33. It is a rare occasion when one sees Ephesian 5:22-33 written in its proper context. It is amazing to me that Bible teachers, who should know better, often lift out and expound upon verses 22-33, while leaving behind the verse just previous, verse 21, which is of utmost importance to the totality of this portion of Scripture.

To be completely accurate one needs to go back to the beginning of Ephesians 5 and get the full picture of what Paul is saying to the Ephesians. In fact, this particular teaching does not stop at the end of chapter 5, but goes on to the tenth verse of chapter 6 to complete Paul's thoughts.

In these chapters he is telling the Ephesian Christians how they are to conduct their lives now that they are children of light and not children of darkness. There were specific areas in which there needed to be drastic changes.

This crucial portion of Scripture, as it relates to the women's issue, actually begins with verse 18, where Paul says, *"Do not get drunk with wine, but be filled with the Spirit."* He then moves on, in verses 19-21, to describe how one who is filled with the Spirit will respond. They will speak to one another in psalms and hymns; they will sing and make melody in their heart; they will give thanks for all things; and they will be subject to one another in the fear of Christ.

Then in what follows, from verse 22 through 6:10, he deals with three separate areas of society in which there has been gross inequity and abuse of power: husbands and wives, fathers and sons, and slaves and masters.

The pivotal verse is verse 21, the one that is so often omitted when quoting the portion in Ephesians 5 having to do with the submission issue. It says, *". . . be subject to one another in the fear of Christ."* One simply can not single out one portion of society, that is, one-half of the human race, and say that this Scripture tells them, and them alone, to submit. Rather, Paul is saying there needs to be a general spirit of submission to one another on every level: wives to husbands, husbands to wives; children to parents, fathers to children; and slaves to masters, masters to slaves.

To quote Ephesians 5:22-33 without including verse 21 is a gross exegetical error (Rule #3, Rule of Context, p. 49). Furthermore, to quote verse 22 in its original state would not make sense without verse 21, because the verb in the Greek text was not included in verse 22. The original text of verse 22 actually reads, *"wives to your own husbands as to the Lord."* So when most of our translations say, *"Wives,* (be subject) *to your own husbands,"* they're having to insert words that are not in the original in order to make a complete sentence.[1]   When quoting this portion in Ephesians, verse 21 must be included to give true integrity to the subject.

Marriage in the First Century

To understand the necessity for Paul's Ephesians discourse here, one needs to understand what marriage was like in the First Century. Marriages in three nationalities were represented and addressed in this chapter. There was the Jewish marriage, the Greek marriage, and the Roman marriage.

Marriage was held in high regard among the Jewish people. It was thought that everyone should be married. However, the Old Testament laws to protect women had been ignored, or made ineffective, making it very easy for a man to obtain a divorce. All the wife had to do to constitute grounds for divorce was to burn his dinner, go out with her head uncovered, or speak negatively about his parents. Or, if a Jewish husband saw a prettier woman he wanted to marry, he was free to do so. Women could not divorce, but if a wife chose to leave her husband, she had to leave her children with him. In general, women were considered inferior to men and held in very low esteem.[2] They were considered possessions on the level of animals and had no voice whatsoever in the relationship.

Among the Greeks it was considered necessary to marry in order to provide legitimate heirs to a man's property, but marriage was not considered particularly satisfying otherwise. Women were very young, about 14, when they married. The men were much older, in the neighborhood of thirty-seven years old. Since it was the responsibility of a Greek wife to manage her husband's household affairs, it was considered prudent for a man to marry a very young girl so he could teach her the way he wished his household to be managed. Eroticism being part of Greek life, a husband did not need a wife for companionship, love, or sexual fulfillment. It was not considered immoral for husbands to have affairs. However, there were serious penalties for an adulterous wife. The wife's legal position to her husband was much like a child or a slave. She actually went from the rule of her father to the rule of her husband and, if her husband died, to the rule of her son, if he was old enough. Consequently, in the Greek marriage, there was little common ground between the husband and the wife.[3]

The Roman marriage was much like the Greek, but Roman wives had more freedom. They could own property, and a wife could obtain a divorce. However, the power over the family clearly rested in the hands of the husband and/or father. Some wives, especially among the upper class, were able to find ways around both the law and their husbands in order to do with their money and themselves as they wished.[4] Many Roman women were well educated, and there is historical evidence indicating that a number of them reached highly responsible positions in government.

Because of the general imbalance in the marriage relationships of that day, one can readily see the necessity for Paul to instruct these Ephesian believers as to how husbands and wives were to relate to each other. Women had been forced to outward obedience. However, Paul needed to exhort them to have an attitude of submission in their hearts toward their husbands (their head) even as the Church is to have a heart of submission to Christ (her Head).

Then Paul talked about the reversal, that is, how a husband was to submit to his wife. He taught that a husband's submission to his wife involved loving her. That concept was totally foreign to that age and society; husbands knew little or nothing about loving their wives. Paul needed to deal in depth with the subject. He proceeded to explain the kind of love a husband was to have for his wife, that is, a sacrificial love that goes beyond what the word "submission" alone denotes. He even went so far as to compare it with the love Christ has for His Bride, the Church; a love that made Him willing to die for Her.

The Meaning of Submission

Submission! What in the world does it really mean? The verb, "to be in subjection," is from the Greek word *hupotasso* and means "to place, arrange, or rank under; to subject, to subordinate, to obey; to submit to one's control; to yield to one's admonition or advice."[5] Although the word includes a dimension of obedience, it is more a heart attitude of yieldedness than a blind obedience.

One author has this interesting comment:

> Two words are constantly confused in reference to woman's duties, "subjection" and "obedience." ... The noun "subjection" is not found (in Classical Greek) outside the New Testament, and we are left to infer that it was coined to describe a relation peculiar to believers. Had the word merely meant "obedience," such an invention would have been needless. ... The true sense of the word describes the Christian grace of yielding one's preferences to another, where principle is not involved, rather than asserting one's rights.[6]

When submission between Christians is referred to in the New Testament, it generally means an open attitude of mutual acceptance, sharing ideas, and yielding to the desire of the other, not mindless obedience. Never would one be expected to blindly **obey** every other Christian, yet, Ephesians 5:21 says we are to **submit** ourselves to one another.

The apostles plainly taught "subjection" to the civil authorities or powers that be,[7] however, they were constantly disobeying those powers when they conflicted with God's commands in order to *"obey God rather than men"* (Acts 5:29). They weren't being inconsistent. They simply understood "subjection" to mean an attitude of flowing, yielding, and preferring, or respecting, the God-granted positions of civil authority, not absolute obedience.

In 1 Corinthians 16:16, Paul says: *". . . be in subjection to such men and to everyone who helps in the work and labors."* Now if this meant blind obedience, this would also mean that the men in the church at Corinth must obey women because those who helped in the work and labor of the Gospel included Phoebe (Romans 16:1, 2); Priscilla (Romans 16:3); Junias, whom many scholars agree was a woman (Romans 16:7); and Tryphaena and Tryphosa (Romans 16:12). Those with a traditional understanding would find this command difficult, to say the least.

One can not arbitrarily decide that when the word "subjection" or "submission" is used referring to wives, it means absolute obedience, unless one is ready to place that meaning upon every other similiar reference. And that would be both unbiblical and unthinkable.

The husband and wife, in "being subject to one another" (verse 21) are to place themselves second to the other, they are to honor the desires and advice of the other.

Ephesians 5:23 speaks of Christ as not only the Head of the Church but also Her Savior. How deep our worship and submission should be to Him. If the husband is truly laying down his life for his wife, as verse 25 teaches, he will, in effect, be a "savior" in life to his wife, exemplifying a deep level of submission to her. The response from his wife should be one of deep honor and submission. I believe Paul was explaining a deeper level of submission exchanged between husbands and wives than that which should be between all other believers.

However, Jesus Christ is the master of a believing wife just as He is of the believing husband, and He meant what He said when He said, "No one can serve two masters." All believers are called upon to exercise forbearance, yield one's preferences, and respect one another's opinions and desires, but no one, except Jesus Christ Himself, should be master over another human being!

1 Peter 3: 6 – Sarah and Abraham

Another Scripture often interpreted as meaning absolute obedience on the part of a wife to her husband is 1 Peter 3:6,

> Thus Sarah obeyed Abraham, calling him lord, and you have become her children if you do what is right without being frightened by any fear.

This verse must be looked at in light of the context in which it is found beginning with 1 Peter 2:12 and going through to 3:12.

The key verse is 2:13. Peter said, *"Submit yourself for the Lord's sake to every human institution."* The Greek word for "institution" is *ktis'is* and is used nineteen times in the New Testament. This is the only time in the NASB it is translated institution. Every other time it is translated "created thing," "creation," or "creature." To be consistent and correct in the context of this Scripture, I believe *ktis'is* should be translated "creature" here as well.

Following verse 13, from 2:14 to 3:7, Peter dealt with several areas of society where there was considerable inequity (much as Paul did in Ephesians 5 and 6), but in

spite of that inequity, they were admonished to submit.
They are to submit to kings (vss. 13, 17) and governors (vs.
14). These were not human institutions, but God
ordained. *"For there is no authority except from God, and
those which exist are established by God"* (Romans 13:1).
However these places of authority are held by human
creatures. They were also to submit to all men (vs. 17), the
brotherhood (vs. 17), servants to masters (vs. 18), wives to
husbands (3:1), and husbands to wives (3:7). I don't
believe husbands and wives are part of a human
institution as NASB says. Marriage is ordained of God,
but husbands and wives are human creatures.

Again, this submission spoken of in 1 Peter 2:13 can
not mean abject obedience. Remember, Peter was one of
the apostles who said, *"We must obey God rather than men"*
(Acts 5:29). So even as he teaches submission to civil
authorities, Peter was one who recognized a higher
Authority Who must be obeyed.

When Peter begins his discourse to wives in 3:1, he
prefaces it with *"in the same way."* In what same way?
One must read the verses immediately preceding this to
get the flow of Peter's thought. He has just explained how
Jesus was reviled and suffered yet did not retaliate, but,
sinless though He was, bore our sins in his body meekly
and without threats trusting *"Him who judges righteously."*
Peter is saying, "Wives, this is the spirit and attitude with
which you should submit to your husbands." Then he
used the holy women in former times as an example.

These former times were times when women were
held at an even lower place in society than when this
letter was written. Peter said they, like Jesus, were reviled
(remember our discussion of the treatment of Old
Testament women in Chapter 3) and suffered at the hands
of men. Then Peter used Sarah as an example. Even
though Abraham told her to place herself in two
situations, first with Pharoah and then with Abimelech,

where she could very easily have been taken into their harems, yet because her hope was in God, she submitted to the point of obedience. As God protected Sarah of old when women had few, if any, rights, so God will honor a woman whose attitude leads her to live a submissive lifestyle.

Sarah was one who submitted to her husband's directive, unjust as it was, even as Christ had submitted to revilings and death, unjust as they were. Sarah's *"gentle and quiet spirit"* is given as an example of what pleases God in a woman. But not in women only because in 3:8 and 9, where Peter sums up his comments, he admonishes all to be *"humble in spirit."*

Sarah's calling Abraham "lord" or "master" was indicative of the authority men held over women (predicted in Genesis 3:16) at that time. Remember, with Abraham, God was just beginning to establish His people, a nation into which some semblance of godly order in this otherwise pagan world could be established. That would prepare the way for the coming Messiah Who would restore all things.

One can not deduct from this one verse that God's plan for women was to include blind obedience to her husband any more than one could say that men should always obey their wives because God told Abraham one time to do as Sarah had said (Genesis 21:12). I do not believe this verse negates a woman's personal accountability to God, or can be taken to supplant the references to wifely "submission" with the word "obedience."

In Matthew 23:8-12, we are told,

> But do not be called Rabbi; for One is your Teacher, and you are all brothers. And do not call anyone on earth your father; for One is your Father, He who is in heaven. And do not be called leaders; for One is your

> Leader, that is Christ. But the greatest among you shall
> be your servant. And whoever exalts himself shall be
> humbled; and whoever humbles himself shall be
> exalted.

This was the New Testament humility Jesus was
teaching and exemplifying.

It is intriguing to discover that all the Greek words
for rabbi, master, and teacher reflect the meaning of one
word. They are all synonymous with one another. Rabbi
means master; master means teacher. Those men who
insist on being master, both in word and action, are in
direct disobedience to the command of Jesus.

In Hosea 2:16, God is speaking of the kind of
relationship He longs to have with the children of Israel,

> "And it will come about in that day," declares the
> Lord, "That you will call Me Ishi *(my husband)* and will
> no longer call Me Baali *(my master)*."

We can see from this Scripture that the husband/wife
relationship is not to be that of a master and his
subordinate, but one of mutual intimacy and love.

1 Peter 3:6 is an example of when the teachings of
Jesus and the overall biblical principles take precedence
over what one might misconstrue one single verse to say.

Mutual Submission

So how does submission work practically in a
Christian marriage relationship? Doesn't someone have to
be boss? Absolutely! Jesus Christ, by the Holy Spirit!
Paul made it very clear in Ephesians 5:18 that the key to
joyful, harmonious living is to be filled with the Spirit.

I am absolutely convinced that if a husband and wife
are both filled with the Spirit, walking closely with Him
and listening to His voice, there will be no need for an

earthly "boss." When a decision needs to be made in a family, both the husband and wife need to make it together. Both should go to the Lord and listen for His direction. If there isn't unity at first, they should continue to seek the Lord until there is.

You say, "Oh, brother, that will take forever!" I can assure you it will, if the couple is not being controlled by the Holy Spirit or not willing to "in honor prefer" the wisdom and understanding of each other.

Even when the Holy Spirit is in charge, important decisions should not be made hastily, but only after the husband and wife have jointly or separately sought the Lord. Many impulsive decisions made by husbands without consulting their wives (and decisions made similarly by wives) which have negatively affected the family (sometimes for many years), could have been prevented if this form of decision making was followed.

In family decision-making, a couple also needs to consider the matter of "domain." A husband and wife need to work out together, before the Lord, the areas of responsibility each will shoulder. Each one's interests and giftings should figure into the dividing of these responsibilities. Once they have been established, each of these responsibilities is an area of "domain" and he or she is free to make decisions relating to that segment of their lives. However, even in each one's area of domain, the other is at some time or another going to be affected. Therefore, one should never be selfish in making any decision, but always keep the husband/wife (and children) in mind. However, each must release the other to manage that area of life as he/she sees fit.

As the years go by, husbands and wives should take time to reassess and make changes if necessary. Different periods of life have different sets of responsibilities. For example, a mother who is raising a family and is carrying the load for the children's daily care and other

homemaking responsibilities might find that her
"domain" would change drastically when the children are
grown, and she would decide (prayerfully with her
husband) that she should take a job outside of the home.
This new arrangement might call for a shifting of the
husband's "domain" as well. He might need to help
shoulder housekeeping chores that up to this time had
been in the wife's "domain."

Nate and I do quite a lot of traveling in connection
with our ministry. Not long ago as we were preparing for
another ministry trip that would have us on the road for a
considerable time, Nate came to me about some detail of
our itinerary to get my advice. He recognized that I
would be affected by the decision since I would be with
him. Although we had never actually sat down and
spelled it out, it was at this moment I acknowledged to
him that our travels were largely centered around his
ministry. (I do some teaching at most locations where we
go, but he carries the greater responsibility.) Unless he
specifically felt he needed counsel or confirmation, the
travel decisions were his "domain."

Conversely, things having to do with the running of
the house are in my "domain," and I am free to make
decisions and keep it running as I see fit, always keeping
in mind that many things around the house affect him. I
dare not be selfish in those areas. It is often necessary to
confer.

Now suppose there is a family decision that needs to
be made and made immediately. It affects everyone in the
family so it must be made by both husband and wife (and
there are times when the children should be included), but
you are not in agreement. Let me hasten to say, Satan is
the master of haste and will do everything he can to
convince us a decision just has to be made **now**. Most of
those decisions do **not** have to be made immediately. If
God is in the situation, He will wait and give one time to

pray about it. However, from time to time, there are decisions that need to be made more or less immediately.

These are the times when each has to take his/her turn at submitting. Some of these times the wife will have to yield to her husband something like this: "Honey, I don't really agree with that form of action, but it doesn't violate my principles. I could feel comfortable with our proceeding your way since I recognize that you know more about the matter than I do." Likewise, the husband needs to be just as willing to yield to his wife in just the same manner at times when she is more "in tune" with the situation.

A few years ago, our finances were such that both Nate and I felt we could not continue carrying health insurance. For many years, while our children were growing up, we had been without health coverage, trusting God for protection. Now we were at a place where we needed to walk by faith again. About a year after dropping the insurance, the Lord began strongly impressing upon me the need to get coverage again and get it now. Nate never did feel as I did. Nevertheless, because I felt so strongly about it and knowing I am often more "in tune" with the practical things of life, he graciously submitted to my "leading."

Most insurance plans have a 3-month waiting period before your policy becomes effective. Less than a year after our 3-month waiting period was over, Nate had to spend over a week in the hospital and receive care from two different specialists. With today's astronomical costs of medical care, his bill ran into the multiple thousands. He would be the first one to acknowledge how grateful he is that I pressed to get our insurance re-instated and that he submitted to my urging.

However, the bigger decisions of life that greatly affect the whole family such as "Do we go to the mission field?" or "Where do we go on vacation this year?" or "How do

we spend the income tax return?" need to be made jointly
under the leadership and direction of the Holy Spirit in
humility before one another.

I am saddened as I observe some husbands who seem
to totally ignore their part in Ephesians 5:25-31. They
conduct themselves as if life was made to revolve around
them and their wishes. What does it mean to love one's
wife so much that a husband would lay down his life for
her? Husband, when was the last time you did something
for your wife that cost you? I'm not just talking about
bringing her a bottle of perfume or a bouquet of flowers,
although either would be nice sometimes. I mean it cost
you:

1. Time you wanted to spend in some
    activity of your choice;
2. Energy you expended to give of yourself
    to her when you were exhausted
    (knowing full well she was equally as
    exhausted and yet on-going household
    demands forced her to keep going);
3. Sacrificing some gadget you had been
    wanting in order that you could buy
    something for her instead knowing your
    budget couldn't afford both; or
4. Your comfort, in order to increase hers.

It is interesting to me that some husbands seem to
think it was written in their marriage vows that they be
allowed time to "play," that is, participate in some activity
just for the fun of it even though this takes them away
from the home and children for hours at a time. I am not
opposed to that (within reason). I think it is great when a
husband can have a good time "unwinding" at some sport
or activity with his friends. The question I have is, is he
equally as concerned that his wife have a comparable
amount of time away from the responsibility and pressure
of home and children? This involves more than just being

there in body so that the children are not alone. It involves stepping in and filling the "gap" left by mom's absence, such as getting dinner started (or finished as the case may be), helping with homework, or lovingly tucking them in at bedtime. It seems to me that if that didn't fall into the category of mutual submission (or if a husband couldn't accept that scriptural understanding) that it certainly would fall into the category of laying down his life for his wife as taught in Ephesians 5:25.

Undoubtedly the underlying reasons for this one-sided thinking are:

1. The erroneous interpretation and translation of the Scriptures as it relates to the woman and why God placed her on this earth; and
2. The license the traditional teaching, subconsciously, gives men to insist on having their way.

I am afraid that many husbands don't have the kind of love for their wives that would lead them to lay down their lives for them.

As husbands allow God to reveal His will to them in this area of their marriages, it will take real humility to acknowledge it and courage and discipline to make the appropriate adjustments.

All of us, both husbands and wives, need to re-evaluate our reasons for marriage. Was it just to get love, affection, sex, security, companionship; or was it to give and share these, with a desire to see one's spouse become all God has called him/her to be?

The "Weaker Vessel"

In 1 Peter 3:7, speaking to husbands, Peter admonishes them to exercise restraint, not authority, towards their wives, living with them *as with a weaker vessel.* To what was he referring? He can not be speaking of emotional weakness. Women are notorious for their emotional strength. He surely isn't referring to mental weakness. There are too many female PhD's to support that. Nor can he be talking about spiritual weakness. To say a woman can not hear God's voice as well as her male counter-part or have as close a walk with God is absurd.

Peter is either referring to the fact that she is physically weaker or perhaps is referring to her legal weakness. Even though womanhood had come a long way since "the days of old," pagan influences upon society still kept her in a weaker state legally. Peter may have been saying husbands needed to live with their wives in a way that indicated their understanding of her lot in life. He should grant her honor since, even though society didn't recognize her as a believer, she was a fellow heir of the grace of life.

It is also possible that Paul is using the "weaker vessel" as an example of how a husband is to treat his wife. Vessels were made of clay in Paul's time and although they had little monetary value, they were guarded carefully because of their sentimental value. "Orientals feel that the clay of the pot is analogous to the clay which is our body; the water within the pot corresponds to God's spirit within us."[8] So it is possible Paul is comparing the way one would handle a vessel that was cracked or for some other reason fragile and "weak" with the way a husband should live with his wife – with care and tenderness.

Verse 7 goes on to speak of the honor that a husband is to grant his wife. How can that be done? It has been said that the greatest gift a father can give his children is to love their mother. Make sure your children know that you, father, love their mother. Show affection to her in their presence. Our son Gerry remembers as a boy coming in from playing and very often finding Nate and I in the kitchen "huggin' and kissin'." He says this gave him a great sense of security because it demonstrated to him that our marriage, and therefore his family, was solid.

Speak well of her in public. Don't keep your accolades just for the privacy of your home or bedroom. The public touching of one another, the arm around the shoulder, the holding around the waist, even the holding of hands as you walk together down the street, all indicate oneness. It is very lovely to see. The onlooker gets a warm feeling of the joy and unity of marriage. Your demonstration becomes a living witness of God's intention for husband and wife. (This would not be as applicable in some cultures as it is in the West.)

Show her honor by helping her with her chair as she is being seated at a table. Open the door for her to a building as well as to a car. Some may call that chauvinism; I call it honor. Ask God to show you ways to honor your wife.

Whether or not a husband chooses to grant his wife honor does not seem to be an option. Apparently God felt this was a message that badly needed to penetrate the hearts of the early Christian husbands to whom honoring wives was foreign. In fact, He attached a serious consequence for those who failed to comply. Verse 7 ends with: "*. . . and grant her honor as a fellow heir of the grace of life, so that your prayers may not be hindered.*" There seems to be a direct connection between husbands receiving answers to prayer and the honoring of their wives.

In far too many cases today, honoring wives is no less foreign than in the early church. Husbands, examine your prayer life. Have you been getting answers? If not, perhaps it's because God has not witnessed your honoring your wife as a fellow heir.

Understanding "Headship"

By now you are, no doubt, asking the question, "But isn't the husband the **head** of the wife?" Keep reading.

The answer to that question hinges on the translation of the Greek word *kephale* translated "head" in Ephesians 5:23 and 1 Corinthians 11:3, and whether it means "authority over" or "source of life."

In the New Testament the word "head" (*kephale*) is used the same way as the word "head" (*ro'sh*) is in the Old Testament. It stands for "chief" in speaking of Christ as "head of the corner." Matthew 21:42, Luke 20:17, Acts 4:11, Ephesians 2:20, and 1 Peter 2:7 are all referring to Psalm 118:22, *"The stone which the builders rejected has become the chief cornerstone."* To understand that verse one must understand the significance of the "chief cornerstone" of a building when the Psalmist penned those words.

In ancient times a huge stone was used as the headstone or cornerstone to give support to the entire building. The walls of the building were built in such a way that they wrapped around that chief cornerstone, giving the building the support that it needed. Christ is just that kind of support to the Church, binding its members together. Ephesians 4:15, 16 says,

> But speaking the truth in love, we are to grow up in all aspects unto Him who is the head, even Christ, from whom the whole body, being fitted and held together by that which every joint supplies, according to the proper working of each individual part, causes

the growth of the body to the building up of itself in love.

Colossians 1:16-18 reminds us,

> **For in Him all things were created** (He gave life), both in heaven and on earth, visible and invisible, whether thrones or dominions or rulers or authorities - all things have been created through Him and for Him. And He is before all things, **and in Him all things hold together.**

There is that chief cornerstone, again, holding things together. Then those verses go on to say that even as He is the One who holds everything else together, *"He is also head of the body, the Church."* In other words, He gives life to the Church and holds it together. This whole passage is not talking about "authority" but "source of life."

Colossians 2:18, 19 tells us to

> Let no one keep defrauding you of your prize by delighting in self-abasement and the worship of angels, taking his stand on visions he has seen inflated without cause by his fleshly mind, and not holding fast to the head from whom the entire body being supplied and held together by the joints and ligaments grow with a growth which is from God.

Ephesians 1:20-23 speaking of Jesus, tells us that God

> . . . seated Him at His right hand in the heavenly places, far above all rule and authority and power and dominion, and every name that is named, not only in this age, but also in the one to come. And He put all things in subjection under His feet, and gave Him as head over all things to the church, which is His body, the fulness of Him who fills all in all.

But the Church is not there under His feet in this Headship of government, but, rather, is at His side. As

Ephesians 2:6 says we are *"seated with Him in the heavenly places, in Christ Jesus."* Furthermore, in Revelation 3:21, Jesus didn't say, "This is My throne; keep away." He said, *"He who overcomes, I will grant to him to sit down with Me on My throne, as I also overcame and sat down with My Father on His throne."*

All through these passages, Jesus is using the head/body metaphor and is speaking of the "head" as that which gives life to the body. None of these passages refer to Christ's government. They represent Him as the supporter, nourisher, and builder of the body, not Her ruler. **It is in this same way that man is the "head" of the wife.**

Recent scholarship has increasingly concluded, after continued study of ancient biblical, secular, and medical writings, that *kephale* means "source of life" rather than "authority over."[9]

There are about 180 times in the Old Testament when the Hebrew word *ro'sh* clearly did mean "ruler," "commander," or "leader," but the Septuagint translators rarely used *kephale* in translating these portions. They used other Greek words that more accurately defined "chief" when meaning a person of authority.

> *Kephale* would have been the natural word to use in all the 180 instances if the word had been commonly understood to mean "leader or chief." Its rare usage indicates that translators knew that *kephale* did not carry this meaning.[10]

Furthermore,

> Examination of the seven passages where Paul used *kephale* in reference to Christ indicates that, when they are read with common Greek meanings of *kephale*, we see a more exalted Christ than when we read "head" primarily with the meaning of "authority over".[11]

Colossians 2:19 points to Christ as the source of life. Ephesians 4:15, 16 emphasize the unity of head and body and present Christ as the nourisher and source of growth.

Just as Christ personally brings His Church to perfection (Ephesians 4:11-13) by means of the five-fold ministry (apostle, prophet, evangelist, pastor, teacher) *"for the equipping of the saints for the work of service, to the building up of the body of Christ,"* so the husband's desire should be to build up his wife until she becomes all God intended her to be.

There is a certain energy a husband is to infuse into his wife. Remember the last time you went to a party and there was one, or perhaps two people, who brought "life" to the party, and without them it would have been rather boring and dull? In fact, they were even referred to as the "life of the party." There was an influence they brought to the party that sparked life and vibrancy and joy.

Life is not a party, certainly, but there is an energizing element that the husband is to infuse into his wife that gives life to her and results in her being joyfully fulfilled and released to become all God intended for her to become as an individual. This is an extremely vital ingredient in any marriage.

It has been said, and I believe rightly so, that the wife and mother sets the tone or atmosphere for the home. After all, this is her domain given her in Scripture (see pgs. 114-16), so she naturally will exude who she is and how she feels which will strongly affect the atmosphere of the home. However, the ingredient of "life" in the form of love, encouragement, praise, and release from her husband is of utmost importance in helping her be the relaxed and fulfilled wife and mother that will set that tone.

This ingredient is missing in far too many Christian homes. However, before some wife finds herself wallowing in self-pity while reading these pages, let me remind you that even if this dimension is missing in your husband, you can and must find your fulfillment in Jesus. None of us can blame our husbands, or anyone else for that matter, for our lack of joy. Jesus is our joy! It is possible to give up that joy by choosing to walk in discouragement and unbelief, but no one can take it away. Each of us must "abide in the vine" that we might "bring forth fruit."

Nevertheless, the relationship of a husband and wife who have become one flesh must contain this "life-giving" dimension on the part of the husband if the marriage is to fulfill God's overall plan. There is nothing in this that gives him the right to dominate, rule, or control, but only to love, encourage, and release.

Whom Should We Obey?

Aren't we supposed to obey Christ? Yes, absolutely, because He is God! He is **KING OF KINGS** and **LORD OF LORDS!** But that is not what these verses are talking about. These verses aren't dealing with His Lordship as One Who should be obeyed, but with the headship of Jesus, the One Who is the "Source of Life" for His Body.

The Greek word that clearly means authority is *exousia*, not *kephale*. Christ's authority over the Church and over the world is established in other passages of Scripture which use this Greek word *exousia*. Some examples are:

> "But in order that you may know that the Son of Man has **authority** on earth to forgive sins" – then He said to the paralytic, "Rise, take up your bed, and go home" (Matthew 9:6).

> And Jesus came up and spoke to them, saying, "All **authority** has been given to Me in heaven and on earth " (Matthew 28:18).

> For just as the Father has life in Himself, even so He gave to the Son also to have life in Himself; and He gave Him **authority** to execute judgment, because He is the Son of Man (John 5:26, 27).

In all three of these passages, the Greek word used is *exousia*, a word that does carry a clear meaning of authority.

However, a husband is not King of Kings and should not take Christ's position as lord of his wife. A woman must answer to her spiritual Master in exactly the same way as a man must. A husband, as the matrimonial head, is a fellow-servant of the King and the one to whom God has given the responsibility of infusing into his wife the fullest life possible.

Jesus, in Matthew 20:25-28, made it very clear how fellow-disciples were to relate to one another. He said the Gentiles exercised authority over one another, but that it was not to be so among His followers. Rather, *"whoever would be first let him be your servant."* This is the key to every relationship.

Philippians 2:3-8 admonishes,

> Do nothing from selfishness or empty conceit, but **with humility of mind let each of you regard one another as more important than himself**; do not merely look out for your own personal interests, but also for the interests of others. Have this attitude in yourselves which was also in Christ Jesus, who, although He existed in the form of God, did not regard equality with God a thing to be grasped, but emptied Himself, taking the form of a bondservant, and being made in the likeness of men. And being found in appearance as a man, He humbled Himself by becoming obedient to the point of death, even death on a cross.

Jesus is the perfect example of One Who came to serve mankind, unworthy as we are. The problem with humanity, and even the Body of Christ today, is that there is more interest in having authority over people — that is, being "in charge" — than a desire to live in a position of humility and servanthood.

Each of us, as Christians in general and husbands and wives in particular, so desperately need to follow Jesus' example and embrace the brokenness of servanthood rather than revel in the selfishness of being served.

Chapter Six Notes

1. Ruth Tucker and Walter Liefeld, *Daughters of the Church* (Grand Rapids: Zondervan Publishing House, 1987), 81-82.

For further reference: Charles Trombley, *Who Said Women Can't Teach?* (North Brunswick, NJ: Bridge Publishing, Inc., 1985), 151-52.

2. Patricia Gundry, *Heirs Together* (Grand Rapids: Zondervan Publishing House, 1980), 72-73.

3. Ibid., 73-75.

4. Ibid., 75-76.

5. Joseph H. Thayer, *Greek-English Lexicon of the New Testament* (Grand Rapids, MI: Baker Book House, 1977), no. 5293.

6. Katherine C. Bushnell, *God's Word To Women* (privately reprinted by Ray B. Munson, North Collins, NY, 1923), 292.

7. Romans 13:1, 5; Titus 3:1; 1 Peter 2:13.

8. Bishop K. C. Pillai, *Light Through an Eastern Window* (NY: Robert Speller & Sons Publishers, 1963), 95-96.

9. Ruth Tucker and Walter Liefeld, op. cit., 455.

For further reference: "Does *kephale* (head) Mean 'Source' or 'Authority Over' in Greek Literature?: A Rebuttal." This 19-page paper by Richard S. Cervin, doctoral candidate for the degree in Linguistics from the University of Illinois, Urbana-Champaign, is available from Christians for Biblical Equality, 122 West Franklin Avenue, Suite 218, Minneapolis, MN 55404-2451.

10. Alvera Mickelsen, ed., *Women, Authority & the Bible* (Downers Grove, IL: Inter Varsity, 1986), 102-04.

11. Ibid., 104-05.

SEVEN

Shall Women
Keep Silent?

I Corinthians 14:34-40

> Let the women keep silent in the churches; for they
> are not permitted to speak, but let them subject
> themselves, just as the Law also says. And if they
> desire to learn anything, let them ask their own
> husbands at home; for it is improper for a woman to
> speak in church (1 Corinthinians 14:34, 35).

For those who have not been comfortable with
the total silencing of women, the most
commonly accepted explanation of these verses
is that it was customary for the women to sit on one side
of the room and call out their questions to their husbands
who were on the opposite side. This explanation is
acceptable and satisfactory to many people. I, personally,
have not been totally content with it.

If Paul is demanding silence, he is contradicting his own teaching of 1 Corinthians 11 where he allows women to pray and prophesy. This makes the issue not a feminist one but an exegetical one and affects the integrity of the Scripture as well as Paul's credibility.

One of the most important rules of interpretation in our list of rules is #3, Rule of Context (see page 49). It is very important to interpret Scripture in light of the Scripture surrounding it.

The Context of 1 Corinthinians

What does the rest of 1 Corinthians tell us that will shed light on these verses?

We know the Corinthian Christians had written Paul a letter (7:1) and that in that letter a number of issues were raised that Paul needed to address.

In Paul's letter, as he addressed a question or issue that had been raised by the Corinthians in their letter to him, sometimes he simply referred to the subject in question, and then responded to it, as in the following examples:

7:1 — Paul says *"now concerning the things about which you wrote . . ."*

7:25 — *"now concerning virgins . . ."*

8:1 — *"now concerning things sacrificed to idols . . ."*

9:1 — he asks questions to bring up the next subject, *"Am I not free?"* *"Am I not an apostle?,"* etc. He is obviously referring to their questions regarding his being called an apostle.

12:1 — *"now concerning spiritual gifts . . ."*

Other times Paul repeated the Corinthians' erroneous statements and then proceeded to correct, or bring balance to, their thinking.

6:12 — Paul seems to be quoting them - *"All things are lawful for me,"* then he counters with *"but not all things are profitable.*" Then he repeats again what probably was their statement to him, "*All things are lawful for me,*" and again balances that statement with, "*but I will not be mastered by anything.*" The Corinthians were justifying license by their words because Paul had taught, "*Ye are not under the law, but under grace.*"

The portion in question here, 1 Corinthians 14:34, 35, finds Paul describing in some detail how the gifts of the Holy Spirit are to be in operation in a church assembly, and specifically the gift of prophecy. At this point a new subject is being introduced. Paul seems to shift to the subject of women in the assembly.

It is very much in keeping with the pattern of this letter for Paul, in verses 34 and 35, simply to be repeating the words of the Corinthians,

> Let the women keep silence in the churches; for they are not permitted to speak, but let them subject themselves just as the law also says. And if they desire to learn anything, let them ask their own husbands at home; for it is improper for a woman to speak in church.

What follows in verse 36 seems to rebut their statement when he says, "*Was it from you that the Word of God first went forth? Or has it come to you only?*" Then he closes this chapter with a few more remarks concerning prophecy and speaking in tongues.

Which Law

The key phrase in verse 34 is "*just as the law also says.*" Remember, Paul was an educated man. He called himself a Pharisee of the Pharisees. Certainly he knew the law. There is no Old Testament law or Scripture that either silences women or subjects them – none whatsoever.

Check the cross reference notes in your Bible for verse 34, and you'll find no cross reference in the Old Testament. Rather, Psalms 68:11 says, *"The Lord gives the command; the women who proclaim the good tidings are a great host."*

Does Paul have the right to silence that "great host of women?" Inconceivable!

However, the Jews were living according to the *Talmud*, not according to the Old Testament Law. Remember the *Talmud* contains regulations and traditions that had become more important than the Old Testament books of the Law.

In "The Ten Curses of Eve" listed in the Babylonian *Talmud*, the sixth is summarized this way:

> "He shall rule over thee," the wife being in total submission and subjugation, since the wife is the personal property of the husband.[1]

When he quotes their statement back to them in verses 34 and 35, which makes reference to the law, he is attempting to show them that they are still living and operating by the oral law of the Jews or Jewish traditions.

> The great German lexicographer, Schleusner, in his Greek-Latin Lexicon, declares the expression "as also saith the law" refers to the Oral Law of the Jews. Here are his words: "The oral laws of the Jews or Jewish traditions . . . in the Old Testament no precept concerning this matter exists," and he cites Vitringa as showing that it was "forbidden by Jewish traditions for women to speak in the synagogue."[2]

Paul would never have made a statement such as is quoted in verses 34 and 35 attributing something to Old Testament law that simply did not exist. Not only that but all through his letters he tried to free believers from the bondage of the law, not hold them to it (Romans 6:14; Galatians 2:16, 5:1).

By Paul's response in verse 36, he is saying, "Who do you think you are, setting yourselves up to proclaim something as from God that is not supported by Scripture?"

We are doing Paul a disfavor and discrediting his intelligence by accusing him of originating this statement rather than understanding that he was simply quoting theirs. Paul is not attempting to establish the silencing of women in the New Testament Church. On the contrary, he is chiding the Corinthians for their attempt to keep women silent and thereby prevent them from freely ministering as the men were free to do.

Paul released women to speak within the church in this chapter, but did he require them to cover their heads while doing so?

Chapter Seven Notes

1. Charles Trombley, *Who Said Women Can't Teach?* (North Brunswick, N J: Bridge Publishing, Inc., 1984), 30. Summarized from *Genesis with a Talmudic Commentary* by Herson.

2. Johann Friederich Schleusner as quoted in Katherine C. Bushnell, *God's Word to Women* (privately reprinted by Ray B. Munson, P. O Box 417, North Collins, NY 14111, 1923), 201.

EIGHT

The
Head Covering

I Corinthians 11:3-16

A great portion of the Church today has leanings toward male domination, because it feels that certain passages in the Bible, including Genesis 3:16, establish this. However, only a small segment of the Church adheres to the head covering for women as the biblical sign of that male authority. Even Anabaptist groups, who have historically followed this conviction, such as the Mennonites and the Brethren In Christ, are moving away from the practice.

I have great admiration for Christians who live by their convictions no matter how stringent they may be. At the same time, I am saddened by the bondage some of these convictions have kept them in. I am concerned that they are basing their salvation on the living out of these convictions, rather than the grace of God through faith in the shed blood of Jesus. My own church background was one that, historically, was conservative regarding dress, although it did not include the head covering for women. I know from experience how easy it is to measure one's spirituality by how closely one is adhering to established standards, rather than by one's personal relationship with Jesus.

On the other hand, one wonders if male domination is biblical and if 1 Corinthians teaches that there should be a sign on a woman's head acknowledging that domination, why are there so many Christians who do not follow that teaching? Shouldn't we be consistent? Either the Bible teaches male authority and women need to accordingly cover their heads, or there is no biblical basis for male authority, and 1 Corinthians 11 is saying something else.

I am convinced there is no biblical basis for male authority and, therefore, 1 Corinthians 11 is addressing an issue that was a source of controversy in the Corinthian church at that time.

Another of the rules of interpretation is needed here: Rule #4, Rule of Historical Background (see page 49). One dare not separate interpretation and historical investigation. Remember, in our Western civilization we are trying to amalgamate into our way of thinking all of Scripture which was written by and for the Eastern mind. Cultural practices were either referred to or otherwise connected to many portions of Scripture. Without knowing and understanding these cultural practices we can not accurately interpret what the writer is attempting to say. I believe such is the case with 1 Corinthians 11.

Cultural and religious dogma (especially for the Jews who were by this time living throughout the Roman Empire) held strongly to the practice of a married woman having her head covered in public. This was directly related to the male domination tradition. As new believers became part of the Church and were being discipled, freedom from the bondages of the law was being taught. As a part of this new-found freedom, the whole subject of whether or not heads should be covered when praying had become an issue in the Corinthian church. In this chapter, as in 1 Corinthians 14, Paul is responding to arguments a contentious group of believers apparently had been holding onto and which had been related to Paul in their letter to him.

He begins this portion in verses 1 and 2 by challenging them to imitate him as he imitates Christ. He praises them for holding firmly to the traditions he (Paul) had taught them and not yielding to that faction who insisted upon clinging to former rules and regulations.

Next, we need to observe that in verses 3-10 there seems to be one tone followed by verses 11-16 which takes on quite a contradictory tone. It is an insult to Paul's coherency to assign to him the origination of these statements. I believe in verses 3-10 of this chapter, as in 1 Corinthians 14, Paul is referring to the arguments the "contentious" Jews were making which was causing the controversy in the Corinthian church.

Is There a Hierarchy?

Verse 3 is the basis the striving Corinthians were using to support their argument for the woman's head covering. However, I believe their understanding of "head" was more accurate than today's traditional understanding.

There are those who believe that verse 3 in 1 Corinthians 11 is talking about a hierarchical structure:

> But I want you to understand that Christ is the head of every man, and the man is the head of a woman, and God is the head of Christ.

Nothing else in the passage suggests this. The only time *exousia*, which was a well accepted and understood

word for authority at that time, is used in this portion
(verse 10) is in reference to the woman's own authority.
The Septuagint, when translating *ro'sh* ordinarily used
kephale when the physical "head" was intended and
almost never did where "ruler" was intended.[1] So the
Corinthians would have naturally accepted Paul's "head"
as "source" – more specifically "source of life."

If Paul had wanted to convey the idea of a chain of
command, he surely would have used a word that
everyone would have understood to mean authority, such
as *exousia*. He also would have arranged it in proper
order: God, Christ, man, woman.

Also, Paul could not be talking governmentally or
hierarchically because God and Christ are equal in
authority. Even while on earth Jesus said, *"I and the Father
are one"* John 10:30. The Jews understood this to mean
equality because in verse 33 of the same chapter they said,
" . . . *because you, being a man, make yourself out to be God!"*
And Jesus said in John 8:42, *"I proceed forth and have come
from God . . . "* So "head" here means "source of life."

Even the "contentious" Corinthians understood
"head" to be "source of life" and, in fact, were using this
truth to support their arguments since so much is said in
verses 8 and 9 about the source of life of man and woman.
This group of Corinthians were using all of these
arguments to support keeping women "in their place." I
believe Paul, in making this statement in verse 3, is
showing that the Corinthians were using the "headship"
truth as a foundation for their following arguments. In
other words, Paul was saying, "Yes, that is true, but when
you get to verse 11 you will see how I bring balance to the
erroneous statements you have made (verses 4-10) based
on that 'headship'."

> Verses 4-6: "Every man who has something on his
> head while praying or prophesying, disgraces his head.

But every woman who has her head uncovered while praying or prophesying, disgraces her head; for she is one and the same with her whose head is shaved. For if a woman does not cover her head, let her also have her hair cut off; but if it is disgraceful for a woman to have her hair cut off or her head shaved, let her cover her head."

Verses 4-6 are so full of legalism and bondage that it is virtually impossible to attribute those words to the one who wrote, *"It was for freedom that Christ set us free; therefore keep standing firm and do not be subject again to a yoke of slavery"* (Galatians 5:1). Rather Paul is still referring to the arguments of the "contentious" Corinthians.

In the Image of God

Verse 7:

> For a man ought not to have his head covered, since he is the image and glory of God; but the woman is the glory of man.

Paul, who knew the Old Testament Scriptures would never have made such a statement as this. He knew that Genesis 1:27 says,

> And God created man in His own image, in the image of God He created him; male and female He created them.

And Genesis 5:1, 2:

> This is the book of the generations of Adam. In the day when God created man, He made him in the likeness of God. He created them male and female and He blessed them and named them Man in the day when they were created.

Man and woman together were created in the image
(and glory) of God and Paul knew this very well. He was
schooled in the Law (Acts 22:3 and Philippians 3:5) and
would never have taught that only man was made in the
image of God.

The arguments that are presented in verses 8 and 9,
although having some thread of truth in them, are so
contradicted by Paul's words beginning with verse 11 that
one can not attribute them to Paul.

Verses 8, 9:

> For man does not originate from woman, but
> woman from man; for indeed man was not created for
> the woman's sake but woman for man's sake.

These verses contain some truth in that woman was
formed from man and, indeed, was given to man as a
"helper suitable." However, verse 9 must be looked at in
light of Genesis 2:18, keeping in mind the scriptural
meaning of "helper." Remember man was not created
because woman **needed** man, but because man **needed**
woman.

Then comes the Corinthians' statement in which they
attempt to put the bondage of a head covering onto the
women.

Verse 10:

> Therefore the woman ought to have a symbol of
> authority on her head, because of the angels.

This statement is totally contradicted in verse 16 which
we'll discuss later.

Paul's Rebuttal

It is at this point that the tone of this passage changes
as Paul, in verses 11 and 12, begins his rebuttle and brings

the balance to the male dominance arguments that had been referred to previously.

Verses 11, 12:

> However, in the Lord, neither is woman independent of man, nor is man independent of woman. For as the woman originates from the man, so also the man has his birth through the woman; and all things originate from God.

In these verses Paul is teaching an interdependence and equality of man and woman culminating in the fact that we all come from God. He is the source of life for all mankind.

A key phrase here is **"in the Lord."** "Religion," whether in New Testament times or today, contains many "laws," rules, and bondages. But they all pass away when one comes under the New Covenant. To be "in the Lord" is to be set free from all legalism and religious mores. To be "in the Lord" is to be walking in relationship with Him and with fellow believers, made possible by Jesus' shed blood. One's value is no longer measured by who you are or what you do, and definitely not your gender (Galatians 3:28). This means there is no need for any "veiling."

2 Corinthians 3:16 says, *"But whenever a man turns to the Lord, the veil is taken away."* In other words, the veil, whether referring to Jewish law, hardness of heart, or condemnation for sin, is removed when one turns to the Lord. And what liberty is described in 2 Corinthians 3:17, 18:

> Now the Lord is the spirit, and where the Spirit of the Lord is, there is liberty. But we **all**, with **unveiled face** beholding as in a mirror the glory of the Lord, are being transformed into the same image from glory to glory, just as from the Lord, the Spirit.

This truth applies to women as well as to men. Paul would **never** teach the removal of a spiritual veil and at the same time place redeemed women under the bondage of a literal veil.

> It was for freedom that Christ set us free; therefore keep standing firm and do not be subject again to a yoke of slavery (Galatians 5:1).

A number of years ago, I went through a short period when I felt I should cover my head whenever I prayed (especially in public). We were fellowshipping with Christians who actually did this, and having great respect for their walk with the Lord, I began to feel that I should follow their practice. It was devastating to my spirit. Every time we would get ready to have prayer with someone, I couldn't listen to God or pray freely. I was too concerned about my having, or not having, something on my head.

One day the Lord in His faithfulness spoke to my heart. He said, "Joanne, anything that keeps you from freely and openly coming into My presence is bondage. That is not of Me." I was immediately set free! It was not until I was immersed in this study that I came into a clear understanding of this Scripture; but I was set free at that earlier time by the Holy Spirit.

Nature And Hair Length

Some Greek scholars are quite convinced that 1 Corinthians 11:13-15 should not be translated in the form of questions as they are:

> Judge for yourselves: is it proper for a woman to pray to God with head uncovered? Does not even nature itself teach you that if a man has long hair, it is a

dishonor to him, but if a woman has long hair, it is a glory to her? For her hair is given to her for a covering.

There are no interrogative words in the Greek text nor, of course, were there any question marks. And, no, in fact nature does not teach us anything regarding men and long hair. A man's hair will grow just as long as woman's if left to nature. The Bible has several references to the vow of the Nazarite, which included not cutting one's hair (Numbers 6:1-21). Samuel's mother vowed that Samuel's hair would never be cut; that he would be dedicated or separated unto the Lord all his days (1 Samuel 1:11). Paul let his hair grow at one point in accordance with a vow he had made (Acts 18:18).

Nature has never taught the Chinese that long hair is shameful: millions of men in China have long hair. The Native American woman is attracted by long flowing hair on her brave. So it is clearly not a fact of nature that long hair is shameful for a man. Whether long hair on a man is shameful or acceptable seems to be a cultural matter.

Some think verses 14 and 15 could be one continuous sentence. When translated in the form of statements rather than questions these verses would then read, "Nature does not even itself teach you that if a man has long hair it is a dishonor to him, but if a woman has long hair, it is a glory to her for her hair is given to her for a covering." In other words, one can not draw any conclusions regarding long or short hair based on what nature teaches or shows one.

Finally, Paul sums up his whole argument against enforced headcoverings for women in verse 16 where he says, *"But if one is inclined to be contentious, we have no such practice, nor have the churches of God."* The NASB and NIV render the verse *"we have no other practice,"* which would cause one to believe Paul is advocating the head covering for women as being the general practice of all the churches. However, the Greek word is *toioutos* which actually is the word for "such." When accurately translated, this verse wipes out any possibility that Paul is requiring or even advocating the head covering for women.

Now that we have allowed women's voices to be heard in the Church and have "removed" the head covering, should they be allowed to teach or have any leadership role?

Chapter Eight Notes

1. Alvera Mickelsen, ed., *Women, Authority & the Bible* (Downers Grove, IL: InterVarsity, 1986), 101-102.

NINE

Can Women Teach?

I Timothy 2:8-15

*P*aul addresses the subject of women teaching in the church in 1 Timothy 2:8-15. But it would be impossible to fully understand this passage without looking at and understanding the historical situation to which Paul was writing.

Just as Paul had to deal with old Jewish laws and traditions that Jewish converts to Christianity were still clinging to, he also had to deal with pagan doctrines that were being carried over into the Christian church. The mixing of Christian and pagan ideas, called syncretism, was taking place in the church at Ephesus at that time. Paul was dealing here with former pagans who had not made a clean break with their past and who needed to renounce and disassociate themselves from their former practices.

Ephesus, a Pagan City

It is helpful in understanding this chapter to recognize the depths of immorality that prevailed in the pagan religions of the day, especially in Ephesus. Some of the new believers had come out of an immoral, lewd lifestyle. Greek and Roman mythology controlled the society of that day. The worship of Diana (known among the Greeks as Artemis) was the accepted cult of the day. A great part of that worship involved sexual promiscuity – temple prostitution where women were actually the leaders of the cult.

Much can be learned about what was going on in the Church as well as in society by the ancient writings which date back to that period of time. At the time this letter was written, the religion or cult of Gnosticism was on the rise. Early Christian literature indicates that there was a great deal of debate regarding Gnosticism in the early Church.

Gnosticism, which literally means "higher knowledge," had many forms. Some taught that Eve was created first, partook of the fruit willfully and, subsequently, became enlightened with "higher knowledge," thereby becoming a channnel through whom God could reach mankind. Some of the other teachings where women were concerned included liberal sexual behavior with no birth control; the avoidance of marriage altogether; and the putting down of the female role, even trying to do away with it entirely.

Paul Refutes False Doctrines

As one looks at 1 Timothy, it is quite obvious that false doctrine was definitely a problem at Ephesus. Paul was simply addressing the different aspects of that false doctrine. In fact, if one understands Gnosticism and the gross errors it embraced as well as the pagan religion that was coming into the Christian church and all the horror that that involved, it makes 1 Timothy 2 very understandable. It all falls right into place as Paul in verse after verse refutes the gross error that was being taught. This explanation, however, is totally different from the traditional interpretation that has been taught for centuries in many Christian circles.

So let's look at 1 Timothy 2:5: *"For there is one God, and one mediator also between God and men, the man Christ Jesus."*

Remember they were teaching that the woman was the mediator[1], and Paul was saying, *"Not so, but the man Christ Jesus."* When Jesus came in the flesh, He came as a man. Paul was pointing out here that it was a man and not a woman, as the heathen taught, who became the mediator between God and mankind.

Verse 8: *"Therefore I want the men in every place to pray, lifting up holy hands, without wrath and dissension."*

The dominance of the women, having been carried over from the worship of Diana, may have caused a hesitancy on the part of men to participate in prayer. In fact, it would even appear that there was wrath and dissension between the men and women over the participation of men in prayer. Paul is simply correcting this by telling the men that they are to pray and that there should be no argument over the issue.

Verses 9, 10:

> *Likewise, I want women to adorn themselves with proper clothing, modestly and discreetly, not with braided hair and gold or pearls or costly garments; but rather by means of good works, as befits women making a claim to godliness."*

Here, Paul is trying to counteract the seductive way in which some of the women were still dressing. Their whole pattern of life was not totally unlike that which is often seen today in a woman who is converted to Jesus out of a worldly lifestyle. She does not immediately equate her new-found faith in Jesus with her standard of dress. Paul was simply saying that women should dress more discreetly if they were going to call themselves Christians. He was saying that they would have to leave behind the lewdness, the gaudiness, the worldliness that was a part of their former religion. They should dress more modestly and discreetly. It is this form of dress that befits a woman who desires to be an expression of godliness.

The Importance of the Outward Appearance

We women, in this day, need to be prayerful as to how we apply this teaching to our lives. I would not suggest that a Christian woman should look like a rummage sale reject. I'm sorry to say I've seen a few who do. However, I'm equally sorry to say that some Christian women have taken their freedom in Christ too far towards the worldly side, and in so doing, do not exemplify a life of humility and purity.

I am particularly saddened to observe women who have come from church backgrounds where conservative dress was rigidly monitored. As the rigidity has lifted in recent years, the pendulum has swung the other way.

Not long ago I was in conversation with a woman who apparently had come from such a background. She and her husband were involved in Christian ministry. She made a comment which indicated her understanding of the release of women meant women were now free to wear earrings. Observing her appearance, it was obvious that along with the freedom to wear earrings (and hers were huge) came the freedom to wear long acrylic nails, over-done make-up, and excessive jewelry. Her appearance struck me as being more gaudy than godly.

Thank God, a woman is free to dress as she feels led of the Lord and not as she is told by a certain church or group. However, one whose desire is to exemplify godliness needs to be very prayerful in setting her own standards.

So what should be our philosophy of dress? Here's mine. A Christian woman should not dress to call attention to herself but should dress in such a way that if anyone looks her way, what they see will be both pleasing and attractive. Remember, even though God looks on the heart, man(kind) **does** look on the outward appearance (1 Samuel 16:7). This involves color (yes, even a little on the face) that is properly coordinated; hair that is well groomed; styles at least in keeping with the decade (not necessarily the last word in fashion); nylons when appropriate; and shoes that are clean and polished. It should also include well-groomed nails which may or may not be polished and might include some tastefully-added jewelry.

There will be those who will argue that their budget does not allow for such detail. Everything I have mentioned above can be done on a "shoestring." I know. I've done it. What started out to be a necessity in our early married life – going to garage sales – is still a necessity, but has also become my biggest hobby. The buys one can find at resale shops, garage sales, and flea markets is unbelievable, and so much fun! I once had a lady, who knew we operated on a modest budget, tell me that I looked like a wealthy woman. I thanked her and then informed her that the dress I was wearing had been purchased at a garage sale for three dollars. She was amazed!

I have seen some women whose dress and general demeanor exemplify the subordinate role in which their husbands are keeping them. Their lack of self-esteem is apparent. In some extreme cases I'm afraid the husband is

too insecure to allow his wife to look lovely and has
convinced her that dowdiness is synonymous with
godliness.

You don't have to be rich and go to extremes to look
lovely. Neither should one use the excuse of spirituality or
poverty for looking unattractive.

The Instruction of Women

Verse 11: *"Let a woman quietly receive instruction with
entire submissiveness."*

Since Paul was dealing with certain women who had
brought their pagan doctrines with them into the
Christian Church, he, of necessity, had to address the fact
that they had not been properly taught the truths of the
Kingdom of God. He was addressing a particular group
of women in a specific setting and was telling that group
of believers to allow these women to be taught and
instructed properly. Remember, this was contrary to the
Jewish tradition in which women were not allowed to be
taught the Scriptures. Paul was reversing that tradition.
Historically, women would have been told to sit down and
be silent. Paul was saying they should be instructed and
allowed to learn if they were willing to sit down, be quiet,
and learn in a non-disruptive manner and with the right
attitude. Remember, he was dealing with a rather brazen
bunch of women.

The Greek word used here is *hesuchia* and means to
lead a "quiet, non-disruptive life." NASB says *"quietly
receive instruction."* I believe this rendering is more in
keeping with the spirit of what Paul is saying than the
KJV, for instance, which seems to take a harder line when
translating *hesuchia* in this verse. It says *"learn in silence."*
It is really stretching the issue to say that in this verse Paul
was directing women not to open their mouths while

going through the learning process. Dialogue and asking questions are very important aspects of learning.

Authentein

Verse 12: *"But I do not allow a woman to teach or exercise authority over a man, but to remain quiet."*

This is the verse most often referred to by those who believe the Bible forbids women to teach or exercise authority over men. And the modern translations would seem to indicate that. However, it contains a very interesting Greek word *authentein* that has tremendous bearing on the proper translation of this verse. This is the only place in the New Testament where this word is used. The modern translations render it *"exercise authority over a man."* That is not the translation in the ancient manuscripts. It had a totally different meaning when originally written.

When 1 Timothy was written, this Greek word *authentein* was more closely associated with Greek pagan worship and sometimes meant "to commit murder" or, in some cases, to pantomime murder. Human sacrifices were made in the worship of Diana. Priestesses were sometimes required to put men to death, although sometimes it was just acted out. But the message conveyed implied the death of the man. Greek mythology tells of religiously inspired murders of men by women.[2]

Coupled with this, *authentein* also often had sexual connotations which included promiscuous rites by which women went about teaching men religious truths. Proverbs 5:3-5 seems to indicate there is a real connection between this promiscuity and death. This Scripture teaches that seduction by a woman is considered the pathway to death.

Remember, Paul is still addressing the existing problem of syncretism which included pagan practices. It is conceivable that Paul used this word because he was saying, "We will not allow this kind of seductive teaching going on in the Church by these women."

In his book *Who Said Women Can't Teach?*, Charles Trombley states,

> It was long after Paul wrote his epistle to Timothy that *authentein* came to mean "to exercise authority," "to bear rule over," or "to domineer." John Chrysostom (A.D. 347-407) was one of the dominant Greek Church fathers and patriarchs of Constantinople. In his commentary on 1 Timothy 5:6, he used *authentia* to express "sexual license" nearly two centuries after Paul wrote Timothy. *Authentein* had not yet taken on the meaning "to usurp authority.[3]

Paul did speak of authority or superiority of rank in other passages, but there were three other Greek words in the New Testament that were accepted words for authority and superiority:

- 2 Corinthians 10:8 – *exousia*
- 1 Timothy 2:1, 2 – *huperoche*
- Titus 2:15 – *epitage*[4]

All of the above would have been well understood and accepted words to convey the meaning of authority, if that had been Paul's thought. Instead he chose to use the rare word *authentein*.

To say that Paul, in verse 12, directed that women were never to teach men, would be to say that Paul had the right to negate all other Scriptures which clearly give women not only the right but the directive to do so. No one has that right, including the apostle Paul.

No Special Enlightenment for Eve

Verses 13, 14: *"For it was Adam who was first created, and then Eve. And it was not Adam who was deceived, but the woman being quite deceived fell into transgression."*

Remember, some Gnostics were saying that Eve was the first created, not Adam. Furthermore, they taught that Eve willfully partook of the fruit and Adam was the one who was deceived. So Paul was telling Timothy that these Ephesians had it all wrong. He's setting the record straight regarding the Creation order and the Fall so as to refute the Gnostic teaching of Eve's so-called special enlightenment.

Bearing Children and Preservation of Women

Verse 15: *"But women shall be preserved through the bearing of children if they continue in faith and love and sanctity with self restraint."*

This is probably one of the least understood and most often misinterpreted verses in all of the Bible. The best that most traditional scholars can do is to somehow relate this verse with Mary and the bearing of the child Jesus. However, Jesus is the Source of Salvation for men as well as women. It makes no sense to single out women in this verse as the sole recipients of the blessings of Christ's birth.

Nor is it credible to believe this verse to be saying that bearing children in general will be the means of a woman's salvation.

This verse, however, does become understandable when given the facts regarding the Gnostic teaching about womanhood and sexual promiscuity. Given this understanding, there are several possible explanations, any of which are very plausible.

The Gnostic ethics which often took the form of free
love (without contraceptives) resulted in children being
born illegitimately. One possible reading of verse 5 might
be, "Women will be preserved even though they have
born illegitimate children, if they continue in faith, love,
and sanctity with self restraint." That is, if they no longer
involve themselves in promiscuity but follow the Lord in
faith, love, and sanctity, they will be saved even though
their previous involvement has resulted in illegitimate
childbirth.

Another possible explanation is that Paul was refuting
a part of the Gnostic doctrine which taught that women
were to become males[5] and that Jesus had come to do
away with the works of women, specifically childbearing.[6]
Paul was saying that the role of womanhood would be
preserved, reproduction would see to that, but the woman
must also live a life of holiness, faith, and purity, using self
restraint.

A third possible explanation is this. Women who have
been involved in illicit sex and who have had abortions –
and no doubt these Gnostic women had – have a greater
chance of contracting sexually transmitted diseases,
miscarriages, still births and even childbirth-deaths. This
could mean that if such a woman has entered into a life of
faith in Jesus, is filled with His love, and is now walking in
purity, she can claim God's protection.

The purpose of 1 Timothy 2: 5-15 was to refute the
error in doctrine (a combination of pagan religion,
Gnosticism, and Christianity) that was quite prominent in
the church at Ephesus. Furthermore, Paul was
encouraging the women who were perpetuating the false
teaching to settle down and submit to learning the correct
Christian doctrine, as well as to set their moral standards
in accordance with righteousness. To put any other
interpretation upon these verses is to disregard the setting
and situation to which Paul was writing.

So, if this Scripture does not put a restraint on women teaching or having a leadership role, as has been traditionally taught, what examples are there in the New Testament of women who were involved in ministry and leadership?

Chapter Nine Notes

1. Charles Trombley, *Who Said Women Can't Teach?* (North Brunswick, NJ: Bridge Publishing, Inc., 1985), 164-165.

2. Catherine C. Kroeger, *Ancient Heresies and a Strange Greek Verb*, Reformed Journal. (March 1979), 12-15.

3. Trombley, op. cit., 176.

4. Faith Martin, *Call Me Blessed* (Grand Rapids: Wm. B. Eerdmans, 1988), 141-142.

5. Gospel of Thomas (II, 2) Saying 114 (Robinson, 130); Zostrianos (VII, 1), 131; (Robinson, 393). In Alvera Mickelsen, ed. *Women, Authority & the Bible* (Downers Grove, IL: InterVarsity, 1986), 243.

6. Clement of Alexandria, "Miscellanies," 3.45, 63, 64. In Alvera Mickelsen, ed. *Women, Authority & the Bible* (Downers Grove, IL: InterVarsity, 1986), 243.

TEN

Women in

Leadership

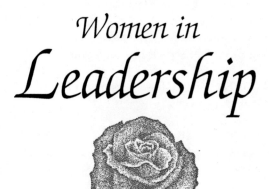

*W*ere women in places of spiritual leadership in the New Testament? Certainly! However, before we look at several examples, we need to look at a very crucial portion of Scripture.

Acts 2 is a foundational chapter for the entire Church Age. In it we have the outpouring of the Holy Spirit on the Day of Pentecost (vs. 1-13), Peter's explanation of that event (14-21), Peter's preaching the Gospel to the assembled crowds (22-40), the mass conversion of three thousand (41), and a description of the life of the early Church (42-47).

In Peter's explanation of the outpouring of the Holy Spirit, he quotes Joel 2:28-32. This prophecy of Joel was quoted in Acts 2:17-21. It is God's foundational truth for the entire Church Age.

Verses 17 and 18 read,

> And it shall be in the last days, God says, that I will
> pour forth of My Spirit upon all mankind; and your
> sons and your daughters shall prophesy, and your
> young men shall see visions, and your old men shall
> dream dreams; even upon My bondslaves, both men
> and women, I will in those days pour forth of My Spirit
> and they shall prophesy.

As we look at this passage, we discover God is
pouring forth His Spirit equally upon both men and
women. All other New Testament Scriptures dealing with
the subject of men and women must be interpreted in light
of this truth: **God's purpose for the Church Age is to
pour His Spirit out equally upon men and women alike.**

Now let's see how God anointed women for
ministry and leadership and how the early Church viewed
women in these roles.

Priscilla

In Romans 16:3, Paul says, *"Greet Prisca* (spelled
Priscilla in other passages) *and Aquila my fellow-workers in
Christ Jesus."* Whenever names are listed in the New
Testament, the more prominent one is listed first. Since
Prisca is listed first in this verse, it indicates that she was
considered the leader of this husband and wife ministry
team. Also in Acts 18:26, Priscilla is mentioned first before
her husband Aquilla, again indicating that of the two,
she had the more prominent role in teaching. Paul calls
them his fellow-workers, not Aquilla his fellow-worker.
They both were well known in all the churches of the
Gentiles (Romans 16:4).

Phoebe

In Romans 16:1-2, we read about a woman by the name of Phoebe,

> I commend to you our sister, Phoebe, who is a servant of the church which is at Cenchrea; that you receive her in the Lord in a manner worthy of the saints, and that you help her in whatever matter she may have need of you; for she herself has also been a helper of many, and of myself as well.

In verse 1, the word translated "servant" is the Greek word *diakonos*. This is the same Greek word used in 1 Corinthians 3:5 referring to Apollos and Paul. The KJV translates it "ministers" and NASB and NIV translate it "servants." Also in Colossians 1:7, concerning Epaphros who took the Gospel to Colossae, the word *diakonas* is translated "minister" in the KJV and NIV and "servant" in NASB. In Acts 21:19 this word is translated "ministry" in all three versions in describing the work of Paul. In 2 Timothy 4:5, Paul admonishes Timothy to do the work of his "ministry" and is thus rendered in all three translations. These are but a few of the many different references where the Greek word *diakonos* is often translated "minister" rather than "servant."

It seems very strange that the one time when this word is used directly referring to a woman, all three translations render it "servant." However, when *diakonos* is used when referring to men, it usually is translated "minister" which denotes teaching or preaching. There is no problem with Phoebe being called a servant; that is what the word *diakonos* means. It seems, however, that the translators were trying to restrict Phoebe to a lesser role as evidenced by the inconsistency in the translation of *diakonos*. She was "a minister" in the same way that Paul was "a minister."

In Romans 16:2 another word is used in describing Phoebe. This word is *prostatis* and is "the feminine word for a person set over others, a female guardian, protectress, patroness, caring for the affairs of others and aiding them with her resources."[1] Yet in the NASB and NIV this word is translated "helper" and "a great help" respectively. The modern translations are not allowing Phoebe to be recognized for the leadership role the word *prostatis* indicates she actually fulfilled in her work with Paul in Cenchrea.

Other New Testament Women

1 Corinthians 1:11 refers to "Cloe's people" ("people" being in italics). This was most probably "the church meeting in her home" and not her family or servants. Historical writings suggest to us that when Scripture refers to a particular woman "and the church that meets in her house," these women were not just hosting the meeting but had a prominent place of leadership within the group.[2]

In Romans 16:7, Junias is referred to as an apostle. Present day translations and authorities are about equally divided on whether this is a female name "Junia" or a male name "Junias." However, a number of the Church fathers understood it to be feminine, including Origen (A.D. 185-253), Chrysostom (347-407), and Jerome (304-419). Dr. Leonard Swidler, in his book *Biblical Affirmations of Women* says, "To the best of my knowledge, no commentator on the text until Aegidus of Rome (A. D. 1245-1316) took the name to be masculine."[3]

In Philippians 4:3, Euodia and Syntyche are mentioned in the context of "fellow-workers." Paul describes them as *". . . these women who have shared my struggle in the cause of the gospel. . ."*

1 Timothy 5:1 is referring to male elders; 5:2 to female elders. A female form of the word *presbyter* is used, although, most translations try to obscure this by rendering it to be referring simply to "older men" and "older women." Likewise, some scholars believe that Titus 2:3, where the Greek word *presbytidas* was used, is speaking of women elders, not "older women."[4] The office of presbyteress was abolished by the Council of Laodicia in A.D. 363, which indicates that at some prior period there must have been such an office.[5]

2 John was written ". . . *to the chosen* (elect - KJV) *lady.*" Many commentators believe that since the church has been called the "Bride of Christ," John was actually writing to a local church and its members. But it is the whole church which is the "Bride" not each local group. Nowhere else in Scripture is this term "elect lady" used. Furthermore this sentence is almost exactly parallel to that in 3 John where he addresses a man named Gaius. It would appear, therefore, that this elect lady is actually a lady who has converts under her leadership.

The ministry of the women mentioned above may seem insignificant compared to that of Peter and Paul. It is certainly true that the majority of Christian workers in the New Testament were men. However, there is actually more said about a number of these women than about the majority of the Twelve Apostles, most of whom are not mentioned after the resurrection.

Considering the Jewish status of women in Paul's day, the number of women noted in Scripture is actually remarkable. Both Paul and John appreciated these women. They were not just the hospitality committee or the church secretaries, as important and valuable as those roles are. They were hard workers in the Gospel with places of responsibility and leadership.

Those who say women should never teach men, based on a traditional understanding of Paul's letters,

have neglected to consider one other very important point.
Many places throughout the Bible women are quoted:
Exodus 15:21, 2 Kings 22:15-20, Judges 5, and Mary's
Magnificat in Luke 1:46-55, to name a few. There is no
higher form of teaching than that which is found in
Scripture. Everywhere a woman is quoted is inspired
teaching. It is equally binding on both men and woman. 2
Timothy 3:16 says,

> All Scripture is inspired by God and is profitable
> for teaching, for reproof, for correction, for training in
> righteousness.

Does "Keeping House" Involve Leadership?

What about women in leadership in their homes?
Do they have any such role? Traditionally we have been
taught that the husband/father is the final authority in the
home. But a careful study of another Greek word used
throughout the New Testament places a whole new light
on that subject.

We get our English word "despot" from the Greek
word *despotes*. It means exactly the same in Greek,
"absolute ownership and uncontrolled power:"[6] as in
English "an absolute ruler; an autocrat."[7] This word is
translated "master" in the following verses: 1 Timothy 6:1,
2; 2 Timothy 2:21, Titus 2:9, 1 Peter 2:18, 2 Peter 2:1; and it
is rendered "Lord" in Luke 2:29, Acts 4:24, Jude 4, and
Revelation 6:10.

Another Greek word, *oikos* is the common word for
"house." When "oikos" and the noun form of "despotes"
are combined into one word, it is "oikodespotes." When
used with reference to Beelzebul, or men, "oikodespotes"
is translated "head of the household" in NASB; "master of

the house" in KJV, and "head of the house" and "owner of the house" in NIV (Matthew 10:25, Luke 13:25, 14:21).

However, when "oikodespoteo," a verb form, is used in 1 Timothy 5:14, a verse specifically referring to women, it is translated "guide the house" (KJV), "manage their homes" (NIV), and "keep house" (NASB). After comparing the different passages that use some form of this Greek word, it becomes obvious that Paul, in these verses, gave the wife/mother a much greater level of authority and, yes, even rulership in the home than these three translators have allowed. It is unfortunate that the translators could not release all wives and mothers to the full authority that should have been given them by a proper rendition of Paul's word.

Does that give any woman the right to flagrantly flaunt that authority before her family? On the contrary! She should be released to: organize her home, plan the meals, set rules for proper care of the rooms, keep the children's time and efforts properly directed with full release to discipline as necessary, and otherwise make sure her home is running smoothly. However, this should all be done in the context of flowing with the needs of her husband and family. This does not make her a law unto herself, but frees her to flow in her area of domain while at the same time submitting to her husband and family, thereby endeavoring to make the home a haven from the world. A woman can not do this unless her husband takes his hands off and acknowledges the role she has been given in the New Testament, letting her freely "rule" her household.

I have been in more than one home and observed how well the wife has the home and family organized, including five to seven children. These were capable women. However, I noticed a change come over them when the husband was around. These wives went from running a house like clockwork to not being able to make

simple decisions, such as what silverware to use or
whether or not to put the baby to bed. It didn't take a
genius to figure out that in those homes it didn't matter
how well she had things under control in the husband's
absence, when he arrived on the scene her domain was
taken away from her. Scripture does not support this
practice.

The Proverbs 31 Woman

Proverbs 31 describes the "virtuous woman" (KJV)
or "excellent wife" (NASB) as one who would put most of
us wives to shame by her accomplishments.
However, the Hebrew word *chayil* has, as part of its
definition, words that are much stronger than "virtuosity"
and "excellence" would convey. The word means "to
show oneself strong, to display valour."[8] This Proverbs 31
woman was, no doubt, virtuous (full of integrity,
uprightness) and excellent (she was terrific!). However, to
only use these English words to translate a Hebrew word
that contained so much more, displays a reluctance to
acknowledge the strength, and valour and, yes, even
authority, women can handle.

Why is it that, for some men, to release a woman to do
something where strength, courage, and organizational
ability is needed, would be to destroy their stereotypic
picture of womanhood — weak, inept, quiet? I'm afraid
that, in many cases, it is because of their own insecurities.
In order to maintain some semblence of security, many
men find it necessary to keep women in a lesser role.

Working Women

One of the bigger decisions within a family, and one that should be arrived at jointly, is whether the wife/mother should work outside the home. This unfortunately is often considered by the world as a litmus test as to how truly "liberated" a woman is.

I was very angry in the 1970s when the feminists told me I was a lesser human being since I stayed at home and devoted my time to my family and home rather than pursuing a career. I was a college graduate with teaching credentials, and with a husband in full-time Christian ministry, we could have used the extra money that my teaching would have provided. I chose not to, however, because Nate and I placed time with the children — my being there when they came home from school — above money and things. I did not want my husband and children to come home to an exhausted wife and mother who had taught school all day and had nothing left to give her family.

As a result we lived on a shoestring, but we lived well. We didn't have money for a lot of extras, but we had everything we needed and more. We had a modest but lovely, well-furnished home. We all dressed nicely, and our daughter even had the braces she needed for her teeth. This called for planning, watching for sales, lots of sewing, and in general, being creative.

What is my reward? I could write a book on that alone. I can look back with tremendous satisfaction knowing that I established a secure, well-run haven for my family to come home to each day and that I had the time to give my children the nurturing they needed. I was there for them. Our daughter Beth once made the comment, "Mother, I loved coming home from school and knowing you would always be there."

Is it wrong for a woman to work outside of the home? One can not arrive at a definite "yes" or "no" from the Scriptures. 1 Timothy 5:14 and Titus 2:5 would seem to indicate that home is where the mother belongs. However, Proverbs 31 describes a woman who had business interests far beyond the confines of her home. The important question is, "What does God want for you?" The decision should not be based on what a mother **wants** to do to feel "fulfilled" or to have more money to spend. Nor should it be based on what a husband **wants** the wife to do, because he either **wants** her to bring more money in for the things he **wants** to buy, or he doesn't **want** her working outside of the home in an attempt to keep her in a more submissive position.

The decision should be based solely on what God is saying to you as a couple. Earnestly seek His guidance. And, of course, whatever He says to do is what will be best for the family in general and the children in particular. I'm convinced many wives are working outside the home not because the Lord has led them to or because the husband makes too little, but because the family spends too much.

I know a family in which the husband and wife are both working full-time. As a result, their children spend far too much time alone, the results of which are being evidenced in their oldest child. This child needs more supervision and, in fact, has needed this supervision for several years. Recently the wife was sharing with me a bit of what they were experiencing with this child. She acknowledged she should not be working but added, "I don't have any choice." Red flags immediately went up in my mind. I don't pretend to know all the details of their lives, but I am aware of money that they have spent on things – big things – that are far above the "need" category. Nothing — no job, no career, no home, no car — is worth having or doing if it means the children will suffer to the point of making wrong choices that could affect them for the rest of their lives. The sad thing is that this family is only one of millions just like them.

When parents, particularly Christian parents, choose to bring a child into the world, they should do so with a personal commitment to make any sacrifice, material or otherwise, necessary for that child. No stone should be left unturned in order to be able to give themselves to that child for the nurturing, training, guiding, and molding he or she so desperately needs. If that means less material comfort — so be it.

It is far too easy to look around at the material society in which we live and slip into that mind-set that says we have to have two pay checks. I'm convinced that with a tightening of the belt, a reigning in of the high-living dreams, and a rearranging of priorities, one paycheck would suffice. God would bless those families, and their children will thank them. As someone once said, "No one ever came to the end of their life and said, 'I wish I'd spent more time at the office.'" Why do we have to learn that lesson when it's too late?

Of course, there are the single parent or family illness situations that understandably make it necessary for the mother to work away from the home. Those are situations that offer tremendous challenges filled with lots of stress for those families. While they need to draw heavily upon God's grace and strength, we as Christians need to come alongside with our encouragement. For some who are able, that encouragement might include some financial assistance. "Visiting the orphans and widows in their distress" doesn't just mean going to their house for a cup of coffee.

Sooner or later most couples will be faced with the decision of whether or not the wife/mother should work. Above all, (1) seek the Lord for His wisdom and guidance and, (2) husbands and wives, **be in unity** in this decision. It is one of the biggest decisions you will make as a couple.

Unbiblical Clichés

There are a number of clichés we as Christians use that actually have no scriptural basis. One is that the husband is "the priest of the home." There is no verse in all of the New Testament to support this idea. On the contrary, 1 Peter 2:5, 9 says,

> You also, as living stones, are being built up as a spiritual house for a holy priesthood, to offer up spiritual sacrifices acceptable to God through Jesus Christ. . . . But you are a chosen race, a royal priesthood, a holy nation, a people *(men and women)* for God's own possession, that you may proclaim the excellencies of Him who has called you out of darkness into His marvelous light.

Couple these verses with Revelation 1:6, *"And He has made us to be a kingdom, priests to His God and Father."* One clearly finds that we are all (men and women) part of that holy, royal priesthood. Each of us is privileged to stand as a priest before God in repentance and accountability. No wife can hide behind her husband when accounting to God for some action – or lack of it.

Both parents should accept the responsibility of the spiritual training of their children. Mothers can not hide behind the erroneous idea that the father as the "priest of the household" is to bear the responsibility alone. Proverbs 1:8 says, *"Hear, my son, your father's instruction, and do not forsake your mother's teaching."* Both must accept their own role in the children's training. Because of the time a mother spends with her children and because, in some homes, the mothers are more gifted and anointed for teaching than the fathers, the spiritual training in those homes flows more readily from the mother. (In other homes, the opposite would be true.) This does not free fathers to abdicate their responsibility as described in Ephesians 6:4. However, those gifted and anointed mothers/teachers should not suppress the burden and desire they have to teach their children because of some erroneous idea that the father is "supposed to do it."

Timothy learned the Scriptures at the knees of his mother and grandmother. Susanna Wesley, mother of John and Charles Wesley, taught her children. She gave birth to a total of nineteen children. Although only six lived to adulthood, she spent hours with each one privately, indelibly imprinting on their hearts and minds the truths of God's Kingdom.

Some time ago, I taught on this subject to a group of ladies in Montana. At the close of the session a young mother approached me with a joyous expression on her face. She was one of those mothers who had the desire and gifting to teach her children the things of God. However, because she had always been told that was the father's role, she quite regularly prodded her husband regarding his responsibility, which he had no inclination to fulfill. He, on the other hand, recognized her desire to teach the children and encouraged her to do so. She laughed as she said to me, "My husband is going to be so happy that I will no longer be goading him into doing something that is no more his responsibility than mine."

Both mothers and fathers have a God-given mandate to train their children in the ways of God. Both will have to answer to Him as to how well they fulfilled that commission.

Another word that is taken completely out of context and misapplied is the word "covering." Much is said in some quarters of the Church today about one's "covering," whether implying that every woman

needs a man to cover or protect her, or whether referring
to the organizational protection many feel is needed in
ministry.

The place in Scripture where the word "cover" is
mentioned with this possible implication, is Ruth 3:9.
Here Ruth asks Boaz to spread his cover over her as an
acknowledgment that he is her next of kin. This had to do
with the Jewish custom regarding redeemer marriages
where the nearest of kin to a deceased husband was to
marry the widow and raise up children in the name of the
deceased husband. It had nothing to do with New
Testament church life or the protection of a wife by her
husband.

Shouldn't the husband protect his wife, the weaker
vessel? Yes, there would certainly be times when the
husband should be a protection to his wife, such as
helping to lift an object beyond her strength and ability,
performing a task that would be a hazard to her with her
limited physical strength, and even protecting her from an
intruder or assailant.

Then there are times, when the wife is stressed "to
the max" with her daily responsibilities of home and
children (and maybe a job), when a loving husband and
father should step in and relieve her pressure.
(Equally, there are times when it is necessary for the wife
to do the same for her husband.)

Who Are We to Set Limits?

With all that has been said to this point and with the
biblical references where God released women to be
involved in the Kingdom at all levels both in the Old and
New Testament, who are we to say to a woman who is
clearly gifted and anointed by God for some ministry,
"This far and no farther!"? Paul nor any other New

Testament writer said that. Likewise, we do not have the liberty to say that either.

So what about women in leadership today?

Chapter Ten Notes

1. Joseph H. Thayer, ed., *Greek-English Lexicon Of The New Testament* (Grand Rapids: Baker Book House, 1981), ref. 4368.

2. Richard and Catherine Kroeger, *Women Elders . . . Sinners or Servants?* (100 Witherspoon Street, Louisville, KY 40202-1396: Council on Women and the Church, The United Presbyterian Church in the U.S.A., 1981), 10-11.

For further reference:

Faith Martin, *Call Me Blessed* (Grand Rapids: Wm. B. Eerdmans, 1988), 19.

Charles Trombley, *Who Said Women Can't Teach?* (North Brunswick, NJ: Bridge Publishing, Inc., 1985), 189.

3. Leonard Swidler, *Biblical Affirmation of Women* (Philadelphia: Westminster Press, 1979), 299.

4. Kroeger, op. cit., 11.

For further reference: R. K. McGregor Wright, *A Response to the Danvers Statement* (Minneapolis, MN 55404: Christians for Biblical Equality, 1989), 9-11.

5. Katherine C. Bushnell, *God's Word to Women* (privately reprinted by Ray B. Munson, P. O. Box 417, North Collins, NY 14111, 1923), 244.

6. Thayer, op. cit., ref. 1203.

7. Clarence L. Barnett, ed., *The American College Dictionary* (New York: Random House, 1951), 329.

8. *Gesenius' Hebrew and Chaldee Lexicon to the Old Testament* (Grand Rapids: Baker Book House, 1979), ref. 2428.

ELEVEN

Women Throughout
Church History

*L*ooking back in history we see how God has
used women throughout the centuries, in spite
of the obstacles they have had to overcome. We
also observe the way different segments of the Church
have fluctuated in their attitudes toward women in
ministry.

Early Centuries

Following the recorded New Testament letters which
tell us of the development of the early Church and the role
that women played, women continued to occupy a
prominent place in the Church. ". . . even limited
historical evidence witnesses to the fact that the ministry

of women flourished during the first six hundred years of Christianity."[1]

Several writings in the early Church indicate that there was even an office of female elder until it was eliminated in A.D. 363 at the Council of Laodicea.[2]

Women's service to God took the form of poverty in the Fourth to Eighth centuries. There were a number of women, not the least of whom was Constantine's mother, who gave up their wealth and nobility to go into the hearts of the cities that they might minister to the poor. As this ministry developed, other women joined them. A simple garb was developed, and before long an order was formed which became the beginning of various Roman Catholic orders of nuns. Their influence was felt mostly by the poor and the women who joined their efforts. Man's leadership in the Church was in no way threatened.

In the Eastern Orthodox Church there was an ordained office of woman deacon — an equivalent to the male deacon — that was quite active from the early Church at least until 1200 A.D. They had a full range of ministries: traveling, evangelism, pastoral care, ministering to the poor and needy, preparing women for adult baptism, assisting the bishop, leading the female portion of the congregation, and founding and overseeing monasteries. In recent years, the Orthodox Church has been moving toward restoring this office.[3]

13th - 18th Centuries

In 1212, the female arm of the Franciscans was founded by **Clare of Sciffi.**

> Clare was only a teenager when she first heard Francis of Assisi preach. His message was compelling, and with his assistance she fled the security and wealth of her noble family and took a vow to live her life in

the service of Christ. Soon afterward the order of Poor Clares (or Clarisses) was officially organized and she headed that order for some forty years.[4]

The most famous of all medieval Church women was **Catherine of Siena** who lived during the 1300s. As a very young child she made a vow of virginity and, though coming from a large family (twenty-five children), managed to find time to spend in contemplation. As she grew older, not only did she dedicate her life and ministry to the poor, sick, and dying, but she fought ardently against the corruption and immorality that existed within the Catholic Church.

During the 1600-1700s, the mystics became quite prominent. **Madam Jeanne Guyon** was a French mystic who, although a Catholic, had a good deal of influence among the Protestants. Because of this, she suffered condemnation by the Catholic Church officials. John Wesley called her a true woman of holiness.

Susanna Wesley is an example of a woman whose ministry was directed to men as well as women — a practice not acceptable in that day. She was a woman of tremendous discipline. Her husband Samuel was away from the home much of the time. They did not agree on the law of Divine Right of Succession to the British throne which caused quite a rift between them. Their marriage was not very smooth, and Susanna was virtually left alone to raise the children for extended periods of time.

During one of those times, the Wesleys were still living in the parsonage of the parish which Samuel was supposedly pastoring. Susanna had become known for the excellent job she was doing in teaching her own children the things of God. As a result, people started coming to her home for teaching — women first and then men. The man who was preaching in Samuel's absence was not nearly as interesting to listen to as Susanna, and that word got around. She had as many as two hundred people coming to her home. At one point, Samuel came home and told her she had to stop these meetings. Although she was not trying to assert "women's rights," she felt she could not deny her God-given gift to teach the people who were begging her to continue. So she continued.

More and more women began taking on the role of teaching. The early Sunday School movement, originally founded in England in the 1780s by Robert Raikes, had more women than men teaching the classes. Although their teaching met with much opposition, there is little evidence that this in any way discouraged them from continuing.

Nineteenth Century

When **Joanna Bethune** and her husband felt it was time to organize a similar Sunday School movement in America, he began contacting businessmen in an attempt to stir up interest. This not being successful, he encouraged Joanna to go ahead with some of her female friends. This she did in January, 1816, forming the Female Union for the Promotion of Sabbath Schools. However, the men, not wanting to be outdone, met and formed their own New York Sunday School Union just one week later under the leadership of Joanna's husband. Before long the Female Union for the Promotion of Sabbath Schools became just an auxiliary of the New York Sunday School Union.[5]

In the mid-1800s, **Charles Finney** was one of the first to permit women to pray and testify in public. The door to public ministry for women was slowly beginning to open.

About that same time, women began writing hymns. Some of the greatest hymns that have blessed the Church were written by women. These include "Just As I Am," "Take My Life and Let It Be," and "I Gave My Life for Thee." **Fanny Crosby**, one of the best known and best loved song writers of all times, wrote over nine thousand hymns including "Blessed Assurance," "Rescue the Perishing," and "I Am Thine, Oh Lord." Preachers and theologians who wouldn't think of allowing a woman to stand up in a pulpit, would sing these songs every week and be blessed by them.

Also in the Nineteenth Century, women began to be full-fledged preachers. Some of them began talking about having been "called" to preach, and they didn't know what to do with it.

There were three well-known women of that time. One was **Phoebe Palmer** who was called the mother of the Holiness Movement. The other two were **Hannah Whitall Smith**, who is known for her devotional classic, *The Christian's Secret of a Happy Life*, which was published in 1875; and **Catherine Booth**.

Catherine Booth, wife of William Booth, was a very interesting woman. We usually think of William Booth as being the founder of the Salvation Army. We hear very little about the fact that Catherine was every bit as involved in starting the Army as was William. They founded it together.

Catherine's preaching began one Sunday morning in her husband's church where there were about one thousand in attendance. God spoke to her and told her she was to get up and say something when her husband finished preaching. In obedience to the Lord, she did. What came forth from her mouth was so anointed that upon completion of her remarks, William got up and promptly announced, "Catherine will be preaching tonight." This was the beginning of her preaching ministry, and she was so fulfilled in it that her only regret was that she had waited so long.[6]

Contrary to other women who just wanted to preach, Catherine was committed to seeing women released to an equal status with men in every area of life. It was said that she made William agree to their marriage being an egalitarian marriage before she would agree to marry him.[7]

The Salvation Army welcomed women. In fact, the Foundation Deed submitted in 1875 included the following clause:

> Nothing shall authorize the conference to take any course whereby the right of females to be employed as evangelists or class leaders shall be impeded or destroyed or which shall render females ineligible for any office or deny to them the right to speak and vote at all or any official meetings of which they may be members.[8]

So confident was William Booth in the ministry of women that he made the statement, "My best men are women."[9] The Army met with much opposition and was literally scorned by virtually every segment of society during its early years. This gradually changed, but as the Army gained the desired respectability, the role of women declined. (Recent years have seen a restoration of the role of women in the Salvation Army.)

This seems to have been the pattern in other movements as well. As men moved into leadership, women found themselves slowly relegated to non-leadership roles.

During the Nineteenth Century, cults were being founded by women — Christian Science by **Mary Baker Eddy** and the Shakers by **Mother Ann Lee**. **Ellen G. White** was another prominent woman who was the prophetess of Seventh-day Adventism.

There are those who would say this indicates that women have a weakness for sects or cults. History does not prove this to be true as the majority of the many sects in existence today, including the Mormons, Jehovah's Witnesses, The Way, and the Children of God, were founded by men. However, because of the male domination that was firmly rooted in the institutional Church, women who had a desire to be involved in meaningful ministry found much more openness in these movements developing on the fringes.

The Church And Women Today

In the late Nineteenth and early Twentieth Centuries, the established denominations would not tolerate women ministering from the pulpit, whereas the emerging Holiness and Pentecostal movements were just the opposite. They were open and ready to accept women in ministry.

Although the Holiness movement is still relatively open to women ministers today, the positions of the mainline denominations and much of the Pentecostal movement have reversed. Partly due to the Feminist Movement, mainline churches have been forced to work through this issue, deal with it, and are now much more open to women ministers, even the practice of ordaining women. However, in many charismatic churches, there is a great deal of reluctance, even deep antagonism, towards women being involved in a preaching/leadership ministry.

However, God's plan for women's involvement in the work of the Kingdom has been emerging. It will continue to grow as the restoration of women's God-ordained status in life comes to fruition.

As for modern-day women who have been greatly used of God, there are several that deserve to be recognized. **Aimie Semple McPherson** founded the Church of the Foursquare Gospel. **Henrietta Mears** founded Gospel Light Publications and the Hollywood Christian Group, was director of Christian Education at Hollywood Presbyterian Church, and developed Forest Home Conference Center. She was one of the most influencial Christian women of the mid-Twentieth Century. **Kathryn Kuhlman** was well-known for her thirty-year healing ministry. **Vonette Bright** has played a major role in the present-day, world-wide prayer movement. **Joy Dawson's** *Steps to Intercession* and prophetic-teaching ministry around the world has affected countless Christians.   *Nanci Smith*

These women, along with many others who could be mentioned, were and are, living proof that when God places His hand upon a woman with a specific ministry in mind, no human hand can stop her.

Chapter Eleven Notes

1. Ruth Tucker and Walter Liefeld, Daughters of the Church (Grand Rapids: Zondervan Publishing House, 1987), 90.

2. This can be verified by checking the following: Katherine C. Bushnell, *God's Word to Women* (privately reprinted by Ray B. Munson, P. O. Box 417, North Collins, NY 14111, 1923), 244; R. K. McGregor Wright, *A Response to the Danvers Statement* (St. Paul, MN: Christians for Biblical Equality, 1989), 11; and Richard and Catherine Kroeger, *Women Elders . . . Sinners or Servants?* (100 Witherspoon Street, Louisville, KY: Council on Women and the Church, The United Presbyterian Church in the U. S. A., 1981), 11.

3. Kyriaki Karidoyanes FitzGerald, *Women Deacons in the Orthodox Church* (Brookline, MA: Holy Cross Orthodox Press, 1998).

4. Tucker and Liefeld, 14, 155.

5. Ibid., 249-250.

6. Ibid., 264.

7. Ibid., 265.

8. Ibid., 265-266.

9. Ibid., 266.

TWELVE

What Should Our
Response Be?

*I*t is important to spend time considering how one should respond to truth such as this. How does one receive this releasing revelation and teaching?

Response of Women

If God has been speaking to you as you have been reading this book and you believe He is in the process of revealing truth to you, do your own study of the Bible until God assures you of His truth. Then allow God to make it yours and to release you by His Spirit to be the woman He designed you to be.

Accept this freedom whether or not your husband, your pastor, or spiritual leaders are ready to agree. You can be set free in your own heart even if the visible "chains" are still on. Many is the prisoner who has found Jesus while behind bars who declares he's freer than he ever was before his physical imprisonment. Rejoice in who you are in God's plan.

I remember as I was getting into this subject and discovering the mutual submission and equality taught in the Word, I began sharing it with Nate. He had come a long way during our married life where women were concerned. In fact, he had made a 170 degree change in his attitude from having difficulty with any woman in spiritual leadership, to himself releasing women to be in ministry and spiritual leadership. However, he was still of the opinion that the Bible said he was to rule his wife. Although his form of "ruling" did not include controlling my every move, he was still the one "in charge." (He still had 10 degrees to go!)

Since Nate wanted to obey God's Word above anything, he was committed to sticking with his understanding. In fact, he expressed to me very clearly one day that he was concerned that I was getting into heresy. However, he agreed to read Katherine Bushnell's book *God's Word to Women.* (Remember, this was the book he had felt I should read and the book that challenged me into doing this study. But, he had not yet read it.) As he read, God began dealing with Nate's heart and his understanding began to change. Until that change came, however, I still felt a release in my heart as to who I was as a woman before God. How my husband felt could not quench that which was God's revelation to me through His Word.

WITH GREAT HUMILITY, accept your position created by God and begin to move in it. Many Christian women believe if their husband tells them to do something, even if it violates their conscience, they are bound to obey. Not so! Every woman will stand before

God and give an account of her own actions. No husband will "stand in" for his wife.

I well remember a few years ago I was struggling over what I thought was a directive from God which was to give away a ring I had recently purchased. Not having much in the way of valuable jewelry, I wanted to make sure it was God and not the enemy robbing me of a blessing. So I said to myself, "Aha, I'll ask my husband. He's my 'head'. Whatever he says I should do, I'll do." (I realize now, to my shame, I was playing a game with God. I have sought the will of God over many issues and situations that were of a personal nature. This was a "cop-out" on my part, but one I thought was justified based on false "head-ship" teaching.)

To my surprise (because "things" mean little to Nate), he said, "Absolutely not. God gave you that ring for you to enjoy. I don't believe you're to give it away." I was greatly relieved and the matter was settled — temporarily. However, I couldn't get lasting victory and that "tug" kept returning. I was willing to give up the ring as long as I could be sure it was God. Yet, somehow, I could not get clarity. A second time I went to Nate with my dilemma. A second time he admonished me to keep the ring. Again, I accepted his word.

It was not until a year and a half later, when I began this study, that the Lord made very clear to me that God deals with me personally as an individual and that I could not hide behind my husband's convictions or opinions. I realized I had to battle this one out all by myself. So I set about doing just that.

God showed me very clearly that, indeed, He had been the One urging me to give away the ring. All along I knew who was to receive it, so, give it away I did! I said nothing to Nate until after the fact. He has never hindered my being obedient to any clear word I had from the Lord, so it was no problem to him. However, with his understanding today of our mutually submissive relationship, under the control of the Holy Spirit, if I were to go to him again with a similar dilema, he would not be as inclined to make my decision for me, as he did before. His response would be something like this: "Honey, I can't tell you what to do. You'll have to ask the Lord." He would willingly join me in prayer regarding the matter and would give me his counsel but would never presume to play "God" in my life.

The release and victory I received in my spirit when I was obedient to God was indescribable. I had been living under a cloud for two years, not realizing that the ring was the root of it all. Had I not been lulled into lethargy regarding the issue by the erroneous teaching that my husband would hear from God for me, I would have "buckled down" earlier, sought Him more diligently myself, and avoided that lengthy cloud that robbed me of victory. (A year later the Lord miraculously replaced that ring with one of greater value. A gift "out of the blue." Isn't that just like Him?!)

Accept who you are before God and begin moving in it. Become a woman of God. Learn to hear His voice. Then when the Holy Spirit tells you some form of action is wrong, you can go to your husband and humbly but honestly say, "Honey, I can not proceed as you have decided. God has spoken thus to me and I must obey Him." If he has a problem with this and he chooses to proceed as he had planned, God will not hold you accountable for the outcome. Don't ever disobey God to please your husband — or anyone else, for that matter. There are many husbands whose shoes I would hate to be in on the day of judgment. I am very serious when I say I fear for them. *"But many who are first, will be last . . ."* Mark 10:31.

This, in no way, gives anyone license to respond or conduct oneself in a disrespectful way toward anyone —

husband, spiritual leaders, or other fellow believers. But one should be able to move in the freedom of hearing and responding to what one believes to be the word of the Lord to them personally. The secret is **humility**. Don't flaunt your newfound freedom, but in humility before God, walk in it.

However, there are many husbands who will, when they observe that you really are a woman of God who hears God's voice, be willing to start praying together about decisions even before they are willing to accept the mutuality of your relationship.

It is of utmost importance that you ask God to search your heart for any bitterness you may have toward your husband, spiritual leaders who have kept you in bondage in one way or another, or men in general. Recognize it, admit it, and deal with it. This calls for true repentance before God for allowing the bitterness to creep in. It may even require going to the person or persons toward whom you are bitter and asking their forgiveness. Humbling? Yes, but an important step in the whole releasing process. One can not be totally set free to be the woman God made you to be while still under the bondage of bitterness.

Although God may lead you to share your new understanding with others, your husband included, don't feel responsible to change their thinking. It is very easy to consider it one's own personal responsibility to change everyone's thinking on any subject about which one has received new understanding. It is not! That always has been, and always will be, the role of the Holy Spirit.

I remember as I was beginning to teach on this subject, I soon realized it was not being received by everyone in the audience. I was really shaken. I had just rather expected that everyone would be just as thrilled as I was at this revealed truth and be eager to walk it out.

Finding that not to be the case, I felt I had failed in my
quest, and the enemy had a hay-day with me for a while.
Then the Lord spoke to my heart that it wasn't my
responsibility to "change" anyone. Rather, that was His. I
just needed to humbly "speak the truth in love" and leave
the results with Him.

There have been a number of times when Nate and I
have come into a new situation and awareness of what I
teach regarding women has preceded me. I don't have to
be in that situation very long before it is obvious who is
ready to welcome me and who wants little or nothing to
do with me. God, in His faithfulness, has "thickened my
skin" and given me the grace to realize that this is part of
the battle.

On the other hand, I have no desire to battle it out with
anyone. There was a time when I was willing to roll up
my sleeves and go head-to-head with anyone on the
subject. God had to do a humbling job on me. I now am
blessed when I have an opportunity to share the truth
regarding God's plan for woman. But that is where my
role ends. The rest is up to the Holy spirit.

Response of Men and Spiritual Leaders

If you have been one — either man or woman,
husband or spiritual leader — who has perpetuated the
traditional doctrine regarding women, I believe there
needs to be deep personal repentance on your part.
If there are any women whom you have kept in bondage
in one way or another, perhaps God would lead you to go
to them, seek their forgiveness, and personally release
them to fulfill God's calling on their lives.

Some would argue, at this point, that Hebrews 13:17
instructs all believers, which would include women, to
obey spiritual leaders. Furthermore, some spiritual

leaders believe they have a right to assert that control. *Vine's Expository Dictionary* defines the Greek word *peitho* used in that verse this way:

> To persuade, to win over, in the Passive and Middle Voices, to be persuaded, to listen to, to obey, is so used with this meaning, in the Middle Voice, e.g., in Acts 5:36, 37 (in ver. 40 Passive Voice, "they agreed"); Rom. 2:8; Gal. 5:7; Heb 13:17; Jas. 3:3. The obedience suggested is not by submission to authority, but resulting from persuasion.[1]

So we, as believers, whether male or female, need to be open to input from spiritual leaders, or other mature brothers and sisters. We need to be teachable, willing to learn. But no one has been given the authority to counter, or block, what anyone believes to be God's clear word to them.

Surely, if you are a husband who has kept your wife in bondage by your unbiblical rulership, humbling yourself before God and your wife will be the first steps toward developing a relationship in keeping with God's plan.

How well I remember the day Nate took my hands in his, looked into my eyes and lovingly said, "Honey, will you forgive me for all the wounds you received from me because of my controlling approach to our relationship." Of course, I did. Nothing brings healing like repentance and forgiveness.

We were then free to re-evaluate and re-work the way we relate to each other. This kind of change doesn't take place over night. It takes time, and we're still in the refining process. Each must be free to make mistakes. We did. But each digression has been used as a learning experience to strengthen our skills at relating to one another as equals.

Our love and respect for each other has greatly deepened. For a number of years, Nate had recognized my ability to hear the voice of God and had sought my counsel and desired that we make most decisions in unity. However, he still reserved the "right" to exercise the authority he felt Scripture gave him, if he felt so led. My respect for him has increased as I have watched him humble himself before me, yielding in areas he would previously have "stood his ground" as the "head" of the house.

His respect for me has increased because his understanding of me, a woman, has been elevated by the new light he has received as to who women are in God's sight. He respected me as a godly woman but did not see women in general as on an equal par with men. This has all been a work of God as we have responded to revealed truth.

Response of the Church

I also believe the Church needs to repent corporately for the centuries of grief it has brought to women. The Church needs to repent for stifling the ministry of anointed women who have had much to offer to the Church and to the world. The world and the Body of Christ have been denied countless blessings because these gifted women have not been adequately released. May God have mercy upon us!

Pray

Last, but not least, pray. God is in the process of restoring woman to her rightful place, make no mistake about it. Be encouraged! It's happening! But, He has to do it. Our role is to pray that the Holy Spirit will be released to complete the restoration process He has already begun.

Pray for the Church of Jesus Christ that her eyes will be opened to the truth regarding God's plan for woman. And pray for those spiritual leaders who are bound by the traditional teaching and are unable to receive from, or release women to minister from the wealth of insight and wisdom God has deposited within them.

God is in the process of preparing His Bride for His return. The enmity between Satan and woman may be the last demon that needs to be slain before that great event.

We are living in exciting days — and the best is yet to come!!

Chapter Twelve Notes

1. *Vine's Expository Dictionary of Old and New Testament Words* (Old Tappan, NJ: Fleming H. Revell Company, 1981), 124.

Bibliography

Bilezikian, Gilbert. *Beyond Sex Roles.* Baker Book House, Grand Rapids, MI 49516, 1985.

Bristow, John Temple. *What Paul Really Said About Women.* HarperCollins Publishers, New York, NY 10022, 1988.

Bushnell, Katherine C. *God's Word to Women.* Privately reprinted by Ray B. Munson, P. O. Box 417, North Collins, NY 14111, 1923.

Cervin, Richard S. "Does *kephale* (head) Mean 'Source' or 'Authority Over' in Greek Literature?: A Rebuttal." Available from Christians for Biblical Equality, 122 West Franklin Avenue, Suite 218, Minneapolis, MN 55404-2451.

Cook, Barbara. *Ordinary Women, Extraordinary Strength.* Aglow Publications, Lynnwood, WA 1988.

Dayton, Lucille Sider and Donald W. "Women in the Holiness Movement." A paper presented at Christian Holiness Association Convention, 1974.

Deen, Edith. *All of the Women of the Bible.* Harper & Brothers Publishers, NY, 1955.

Deen, Edith. *Great Women of the Christian Faith.* Christian Herald Books, Chappaqua, NY, 1959.

FitzGerald, Kyriaki Karidoyanes. *Women Deacons in the*

Orthodox Church: Called to Holiness and Ministry. Holy Cross Orthodox Press, Brookline, MA, 1998.

Foh, Susan. *Women and the Word of God.* Baker Book House, Grand Rapids, MI, 1981.

Fujita, Neil S., *A Crack in the Jar.* Paulist Press, NY.

Gesenius' Hebrew and Chaldee Lexicon to the Old Testament Scriptures. Translated by Samuel Prideaux Tregelles, Baker Book House, Grand Rapids, MI, 1979.

"The Danvers Statement." Council on Biblical Manhood and Womanhood, P. O. Box 1173, Wheaton, IL 60189.

The Greek-English New Testament. Christianity Today, Washington, DC, 1976.

Gundry, Patricia. *Heirs Together.* Zondervan Publishing House, Grand Rapids, MI, 1980.

Gundry, Patricia. *Woman Be Free!* Zondervan Publishing House, Grand Rapids, MI, 1977.

Haubert, Katherine M. *Women as Leaders, MARC.* Monrovia, CA 91016-3400, 1993.

Hull, Gretchen Gaebelein. *Equal to Serve.* Fleming H. Revell, a division of Baker Book House, Grand Rapids, MI 49516-6287.

Keener, Craig S. *Paul, Women & Wives.* Hendrickson Publishers, Peabody, MA, 1992.

Keizer, Walter. *Hard Sayings of the Old Testament.*

InterVarsity Press, Downers Grove, IL, 1988.

Kroeger, Richard and Catherine. *I Suffer Not a Woman.* Baker Book House, Grand Rapids, MI 49516-6287, 1992.

Kroeger, Richard and Catherine. *Women Elders . . . Sinners or Servants?* Council on Women and the Church, The United Presbyterian Church, 100 Witherspoon St., Louisville, KY, 1981.

Krupp, Nate, *God's Simple Plan for His Church.* Preparing the Way Publishers, 2121 Barnes Avenue SE, Salem, OR 97306, 1993.

Krupp, Nate. *Leadership–Servanthood in the Church as found in the New Testament.* Preparing the Way Publishers, 2121 Barnes Avenue SE, Salem, OR 97306, 1994.

Lance, Fran and King, Pat. *Healing the Wounds of Women.* Free Lance Ministries, Seattle, WA, 1989.

Martin, Faith McBurney. *Call Me Blessed.* Wm. B. Eerdmans Publishing Co., Grand Rapids, MI, 1988.

Mickelsen, Alvera. *Women, Authority and the Bible.* InterVarsity Press, Downers Grove, IL. 1986.

Mollenkott, Virginia Ramey. *Women, Men and the Bible.* Abingdon, Nashville, TN, 1981.

Pape, Dorothy R. *In Search of God's Ideal Woman.* InterVarsity, Downers Grove, IL, 1976.

Pawson, J. David. *Leadership is Male.* Oliver-Nelson Books, Nashville, TN, 1984.

Penn-Lewis, Jessie. *The Magna Charta of Woman*. Bethany Fellowship, Inc., Minneapolis, MN, 1919.

Pillai, K. C. *Light Through an Eastern Window*. Robert Speller & Sons Publishers, New York, NY, 1963.

Piper, John and Grudem, Wayne. *Recovering Biblical Manhood and Womanhood*. Crossway Books, Wheaton, IL, 1991.

Strong, James. *Strong's Exhaustive Concordance*. Baker Bookhouse, Grand Rapids, MI, 1981.

Thayer, Joseph H. *Greek-English Lexicon of the New Testament*. Baker Book House, Grand Rapids, MI, 1977.

Thomas, Robert L. *New American Standard Exhaustive Concordance of the Bible*. Holman Publisher, Nashville, TN, 1981.

Torjesen, Karen Jo. *When Women Were Priests*. HarperCollins Publishers, New York, NY 10022, 1993.

Trombley, Charles. *Who Said Women Can't Teach?* Bridge-Logos Publishers, North Brunswick Corporate Center, 1300 Airport Rd., Suite E, North Brunswick, NJ 08902, 1985.

Tucker, Ruth A. and Liefeld, Walter. *Daughters of the Church*. Zondervan Publishing House, Grand Rapids, MI, 1987.

Van Leeuwen, Mary Steward. *Gender and Grace*. InterVarsity Press, Downers Grove, IL, 1991.

Wilson, Marvin R. *Our Father Abraham.* Wm. B. Eerdman Publishing Co., Grand Rapids, MI, and Center For Judaic- Christian Studies, Dayton, OH, 1989.

Woodrow, Ralph. *Women's Adornment.* Ralph Woodrow, P.O. Box 124, Riverside, CA, 92502.

Wright, R. K. McGregor. "A Response to the Danvers Statement." Christians for Biblical Equality, 122 West Franklin Avenue, Suite 218, Minneapolis, MN 55404-2451, 1989.

Young, Robert. *Analytical Concordance to the Bible.* Wm. B. Eerdmans Publishing Co., GrandRapids, MI.

About the Author

Joanne Krupp is the youngest daughter of the late Dr. Harold K. Sheets, a General Superintendent of the Wesleyan Methodist Church. Although there was never a time when she didn't love Jesus, she dates her conversion to when she was twelve years of age.

She attended Marion College in Marion, Indiana, for two years and graduated from Asbury College in Wilmore, Kentucky, in 1958 with a Bachelor of Arts degree in Social Studies (Elementary Education).

She was the wife of Gerald Brannon, a Wesleyan Methodist pastor, until his death in 1959. A son, Gerry, was born to her two months after Gerald's death. Gerry and his wife Wenda have three children and are pastoring in the Wesleyan Church.

She married Nate Krupp in 1961. A daughter, Beth, was born in 1962. Beth and her husband Greg along with their three children live in Salem, Oregon. They are ministering in the business world and are involved in music and one-on-one discipling.

Joanne has had a Bible teaching and discipling ministry with women since 1971, ministering in North America, Europe, Africa, Asia, and the Pacific. She and Nate reside in Salem, Oregon. Their ministry is directed primarily to the church-at-large, emphasizing the restoration of the church to New Testament Christianity, including the restoration of women to their God-given role.

What People are Saying

One of the significant trends in the Body of Christ in our day is the strong release of the female portion of that Body. For centuries they have been held back by wrong interpretations of certain Bible passages. Joanne Krupp, in her book *Woman*, writes to dispell these misconceptions and to set free more than half of God's army.   – Robert, Hawaii

I highly recommend *Woman*. The revealed truth of God's Word regarding His plan for women has set me free from the bondage of man's tradition. I now walk in a new confidence of who I am in Christ.   – Patricia, Arizona

Your book opened the door of my heart and mind to so many important insights, perhaps the least of which, the satanic darkness which had infected my own male mindset concerning women. It certainly helped me to see and better understand ". . . a great wonder in heaven: a woman . . ." Once seen, she is reason enough for us to lay down our lives.   – Jay, North Carolina

As a pastor's wife in rural Iowa, *Woman* brought an understanding to Scriptures that in the past seemed to contradict the very God-given gifts within me. With a new level of understanding and humility came a release and freedom to flow with my husband, becoming a more complete ministry to our local congregation. I consider this book a valuable resource tool, well written and easily assimilated.   – Victoria, Iowa

Joanne Krupp has been an inspiration to me both by her study of the role of women and by her lifestyle of integrity and Christian love. No doubt the truth in this book will bring much needed understanding, freedom, and healing to the body of Christ!   – Cindy, Oregon

Joanne Krupp has brought insight to a controversial topic in a refreshing way. Her research and practical wisdom demonstrates her own walk with God. Her ministry partnership with her husband Nate lends credibility to the message of this book.   – Bev, California

Preparing the Way Publishers

makes available practical materials
(books, booklets, and audio tapes)
that call the Church to the radical Christianity
described in the Bible.

Some titles include —
The Way to God
Basic Bible Studies
Getting to Know GOD
New Testament Survey Course
Mastering the Word of God – and Letting it Master You
You Can be a Soul Winner – Here's How!
The Church Triumphant at the End of the Age
New Wine Skins – the Church in Transition
God's Simple Plan for His Church – a Manual for House Churches
Leadership–Servanthood in the Church as found in the New Testament

For further information, see the PTW web page
at http://www.open.org/kruppnj

For a free catalog and order form contact —

Preparing the Way Publishers
2121 Barnes Avenue SE
Salem, OR 97306, USA

phone 503/585-4054
fax 503/375-8401
e-mail kruppnj@open.org